REVISIONING THE CHURCH

REVISIONING THE CHURCH

Ecclesial Freedom in the
New Paradigm

Peter C. Hodgson

Fortress Press

COPYRIGHT © 1988 BY FORTRESS PRESS

Second Printing 1989

Library of Congress Cataloging-in-Publication Data

Hodgson, Peter Crafts, 1934–
  Revisioning the church.

  Bibliography: p.
  Includes index.
  1. Church. 2. Christianity—20th century. I. Title.
BV600.2.H568 1988   262   87–45894
ISBN 0–8006–2072–0

3902L88   Printed in the United States of America   1-2072

In memoriam
Robert C. Williams

Contents

8   Contents

Preface

In recent years I have taught a course required of students in the Divinity School at Vanderbilt University entitled "The Nature of the Church and Its Ministries." This was an assignment I took on with considerable trepidation since the literature on the church with which I was familiar was rather dull and conventional and the topic had never been at the center of my own agenda.

I was surprised to discover that through the teaching of this course, I quickly became engaged in a number of controversial issues of importance for contemporary theology—issues related to the conflict between traditionalists and (post)modernists, to the prospect of a rebirth of the church in the Latin American base communities, to current struggles in the Catholic church over authority and ordination, to the women-church movement, to the impact of religious pluralism, and to current crises in ministry. I found myself attempting to work out a comprehensive theological understanding of the ecclesial community in light of these controversies—a vision of ecclesia that might function as both a critical and a productive paradigm in the life of actual churches.

My thoughts about these questions have been helped immensely by a number of Vanderbilt colleagues who, along with several visitors to the Divinity School, presented guest lectures to the course. Where I have drawn upon their ideas directly I have indicated this in the notes. I am especially thankful to Sallie McFague for reading with a critical eye and improving in many ways the book manuscript that grew out of my course lectures, and to Davis Perkins and Barry Blose, of Fortress Press, for their helpful suggestions and thoughtful editing.

Another kind of indebtedness is owed to the Workgroup on Constructive Theology, which at several of its meetings has discussed the question of a new cultural "paradigm" and its impact on theological issues. This group has published a textbook, *Christian Theology: An Introduction to Its Traditions and Tasks* (1982; 2d ed., 1985), to which the late Robert C. Williams and I contributed a chapter on the church. Traces of that brief work on ecclesiology are discernible at a few places in this book, which is dedicated to the memory of Dr. Williams.

Introduction.
What Is the
New Paradigm?

The liberation theologians have argued persuasively that all good theology is *situated*. It is called forth by the needs of a particular situation; it is not simply done in a vacuum, as a kind of academic exercise. If the situation does not demand a new theology, our time is better spent reading the classics, ancient and modern, of which most of us are far too ignorant.

What is our situation, as mostly white, middle-class North American Christians? It is not that of the "underside" of history,[1] like the position of Third World and minority theologies. Rather, it is a situation of the "passage" of history—the passing of Western bourgeois culture, with its ideals of individuality, private rights, technical rationality, historical progress, the capitalist economy, the absoluteness of Christianity, and so on. It *feels* as though we are reaching the end of a historical era, since we find ourselves in the midst of cognitive, historical, political, socioeconomic, and religious changes of vast importance, comparable perhaps to those of the great Enlightenment that inaugurated the modern age. Can we speak, then, of a second Enlightenment, a new watershed, a new paradigm in theology?[2]

A paradigm is an example, model, or pattern. As the Greek etymology of the word suggests, an example (*deigma*) is set up alongside (*para*) something to show what it is; it is a model on a microcosmic scale (a "scale model") of a large, complex, dispersed, difficult-to-grasp state of affairs. In his study of the history of science, Thomas Kuhn uses the term "paradigm" to refer to exemplary formulations of scientific theory, such as Copernicus's explanation of planetary motion and Newton's theory of mechan-

ics. He describes major transitions in scientific theories as paradigm shifts.[3] But we can also speak of a paradigm with reference to
a culture or to an intellectual activity such as theology, where it will
be a confluence of factors or elements that determines the predominant shape or pattern of the culture or theology in question. Major
shifts in the cultural paradigm have generally elicited corresponding shifts in the theological paradigm.

As far as the Christian theological tradition is concerned, it is
possible to distinguish three great paradigms: the *classical* (from the
patristic period through the Reformation: the theological "consensus" from Augustine to Calvin), the *modern* (from the early
eighteenth to the late twentieth century: the "Enlightenment age"),
and the *postmodern*. Since we do not yet have a name for our
emerging new paradigm, we simply call it "post-." Of course, the
discernment of paradigms and of shifts between them is a matter of
perspective. From *our* perspective, the important distinctions between the patristic, the medieval, and the Reformation periods of
the church lessen in significance, since these are now all seen as
variations on the classical paradigm, which was prescientific and
precritical. From the perspective of the twenty-fifth century, our
distinction between the modern and postmodern paradigms will
very likely pale in comparison with even more far-reaching distinctions.

The Enlightenment was a period of revolutionary intellectual
and cultural transformation that occurred throughout much of
Europe and in parts of North America during the eighteenth and
early nineteenth centuries, inaugurating the "modern era." It was
precipitated by sweeping accomplishments in the natural sciences
(beginning in the seventeenth century) and by an emerging acceptance of the scientific world view, which among other things called
into question the possibility of special ("miraculous") divine actions in history and demanded that claims be supported by reason
and evidence rather than by appeal to authority. The impact of the
Enlightenment spread to other cultural and intellectual domains,
notably those of philosophy, politics, history, and theology. Philo-
sophically there was the so-called turn to the subject initiated by
Descartes and extended by Kant. Corresponding to this in the
realm of politics was a new recognition of individual rights and
personal freedoms. For history it was a matter of introducing
scientific methods into the study of history and of recognizing the
historical conditionedness and relativity of all human knowledge
and experience. Theologically what was required was finding fun-

damentally new ways of understanding revelation, authority, and truth claims.[4]

We have lived from the resources of the Enlightenment for two centuries. But there are signs all around us that the age of Enlightenment has run its course. Our first task is to become aware of these signs, to raise them to consciousness. This is an unsettling task since the human tendency is to deny change, to retreat into the security of what is old and familiar, to repeat old forms rather than to create new. I shall attempt briefly to identify five signs of cultural crisis that suggest the end of the first Enlightenment and the coming of a new paradigm—a paradigm that we must hope will incorporate the enduring values of classical culture as well as the critical transformations of the Enlightenment into quite new ways of dwelling humanly in the world.

The cognitive crisis. We may distinguish between a crisis in technical rationality and one in philosophical rationality. With respect to the first, the use of reason since the Enlightenment has become increasingly manipulative and calculative. Such rationality underlies the tremendous productivity of our society, but it is now perceived as increasingly counterproductive. For example, nuclear technology has produced the means of total human destruction, which far outweigh its beneficial uses, and the control of this technology is both costly and risky; medical technology, though making tremendous curative advances, has opened up ethical ambiguities that cannot be resolved by technical reason; industrial technologies have resulted in severe disparities in the distribution of goods and severe threats to the natural environment. As Langdon Gilkey says, "The human intellectual creativity represented by the Enlightenment has revealed itself not only as ambiguous but also as potentially lethal."[5]

The crisis in philosophical rationality is epitomized by postmodernist criticism, which is in process of "deconstructing" Western consciousness and its "logocentrism." The first Enlightenment gave rise to a relativizing consciousness, but Western consciousness as such was not relativized. Now there appears no longer to be a universal logos, either religious or secular. Postmodern critics claim that language is nothing but an arbitrary and self-referential interplay of signs embodied in an endless milieu of writing. Mark C. Taylor has shown how the central Western "ontotheological" concepts—God, self, history, book—stand or fall together.[6] The death of God leads to the disappearance of the self, the end of history, and the closure of the book. Taylor claims that this is the result of the dissolving of the binary oppositional terms in which Western thought was couched and which led to its structures of domination. What we are left with, and liberated to, in his view, is an endless, aimless wandering ("erring") through which we seek out the "carnival, comedy, and carnality" of life in each present moment.

The historical crisis. We have experienced in our time the collapse of "salvation history" as the empowering mythos of our culture —the belief, deeply rooted in the Jewish and Christian heritage, that "divine activity, presence, and the gift of salvation have appeared in and through a special sequence of historical events and thus form a salvation history"[7] issuing in the final victory of good over evil. This religious vision was secularized by the Enlightenment, reappearing as a "theory of progress" based on human accomplishment and control of our own destiny. A rival version emerged in the form of the Marxist-Leninist theory of class struggle and eventual triumph of the proletariat. All these versions—the classical Judeo-Christian, the liberal-bourgeois, and the Marxist —have been severely challenged in our time. Natural science questions whether change of any sort is teleologically oriented toward a progressively "better" goal. Instead of a teleology in nature, we find only "chance and necessity."[8] The deep experience of evil in the twentieth century has permanently shaken confidence in historical progress: two world wars, fascism, Stalinism, the Holocaust, Vietnam, Cambodia, Central America, the ever-present threat of nuclear war, the madness of the arms race.

The political crisis. Crucial shifts have occurred in the power and influence of Enlightenment culture after two centuries during which it could not be challenged by any rival force. Now no European nation is a major power, and only one of the current Big Four is Western in inheritance and values—the United States —and its influence as a political and cultural paradigm is declining along with its *effective* military power (despite enormous expenditures). The decline of American influence, and the country's inability to cope effectively with external crises—Vietnam, Iran, Lebanon, international terrorism—have led to a severe crisis of confidence among the people and probably more than anything else account for the turn to a political leader who avoids reality and projects an image of the old America. At the same time, the social ideals generated by the Enlightenment and cherished by Americans —individual rights, political freedom, democratic processes—no longer seem to "grasp" persons in other cultures but are viewed rather as suspect ideologies. They seem to be alive, ironically, only among the dissidents of Eastern Europe and the Soviet Union.[9]

The socioeconomic crisis. Both free-enterprise capitalism and state socialism have become increasingly dysfunctional and oppressive in the postindustrial age. With the rise of multinational corporations, the impregnability of the military-industrial complex, the rationalization and bureaucratization of controls through new technologies, the decline of labor unions, and the rescinding of social reforms, capitalist economies are experiencing an increasing concentration of power and wealth in corporate elites, and a growing dichotomy between the core and the periphery. With the transfer of industrial and manufacturing activity to the Third World, the choice in the First World will increasingly be between low-paying service jobs and high-paying professional and technical jobs. The effect of this on the Third World is its continued marginalization; whereas the Third World was once used to provide raw materials, it will now be used to furnish cheap industrial labor for exported goods.

An equally harsh but different indictment can be brought to bear upon state socialism: denial of individual liberties and rights, censorship, suppression of political opposition, stifling bureaucratic controls, inefficiency and corruption, frequent scarcity of basic commodities, indifference to environmental concerns, diversion of economic resources into an arms race. The two great rival socioeconomic systems of modernity are bankrupt, and humanity struggles to survive despite them, seeking—fruitlessly thus far—for effective alternatives.[10]

The religious crisis. Two factors in the current religious crisis may be distinguished and mentioned only briefly, since we shall return to both: (*a*) the decline of Christianity in the West, its apparent rebirth in Latin America and Africa, and the need for First World Christianity to "pass over" into new and vital forms of faith and praxis; and (*b*) the "present close encounter of religions . . . of a quite new kind."[11] What is new about this encounter is that it is occurring on the basis of equality among the religions, equality of truth and grace, of illuminating and healing power. The former hierarchy of religions, with Christianity at the top, is no longer defensible. The religious, theological, and ethical categories of other religions now appear to many as potent thematizations of reality, and their meditative and cultic practices may mediate real saving power. It is not a matter of abandoning one's own faith but of finding it transformed and enriched through such encounters.[12]

Periods of cultural transition and historical passage such as we are experiencing today are unsettling, to say the least, and I want to call attention to what I regard as two unproductive responses. The first is an effort to stop the process, to turn the clock back—indeed, to turn it back to pre-Enlightenment times, to traditional bases of authority and conventional forms of religious belief. The resurgence of conservative and evangelical Christianity in recent years is symptomatic both of the magnitude of the experienced threat and of the deep desire to recover stable ethical and religious foundations in a topsy-turvy age. I do not intend to make light of evangelical religion as an authentic piety and vital conservative force. But its potential for idolatry and ideology must also be recognized, its tendency to overbelief in the face of the threats and insecurities of our time—a false securing based on illusory absolutes, such as right doctrine, fundamentalist beliefs, nationalism, and patriotism. This danger becomes acute when an alliance is struck between the religious right and conservative politics in the name of restoring a "Christian America."

The second and diametrically opposed response, arising from the postmodernist sense of "irrevocable loss and incurable fault,"[13] is a radical relativism in which nothing is known, believed, or acted upon. I do not wish to make light of the serious, honest, baffling intellectual questions raised by deconstructionist criticism. But the temptation here is to retreat into intellectual games and hedonistic play—a mask for despair, cynicism, nihilism.[14] Ironically, such play requires a stable order as its context, for it has no staying power against demonic absolutes and political oppression.[15]

Against these two responses we must insist both that the clock not be turned back and that everything not be relativized or demolished in the process of passage. The paradox is that there comes a time when in order to preserve the heritage of the past, we must let it go; if we attempt to hold on to it, we will indeed lose or destroy it. But if we are willing to let it go, it can pass over into new forms and assume a new life. The conservative religion of popular culture is unwilling to let go; the radical relativism of the intelligentsia is persuaded that nothing can or should be preserved. But what of the priceless heritage of antiquity, its mediation of truth, beauty, and goodness in the form of religious mythologies and scriptures, literature and philosophy, art and architecture, drama and music? Much of this heritage has already been lost or forgotten in our technological, utilitarian, consumeristic culture. What also of the heritage of modernity, of the age of Enlightenment, its discovery of subjectivity, individual rights, political freedom, democratic processes, critical rationality, scientific method? These are gains of human consciousness which must not be allowed to perish as we make the transition to new forms.

The passage of which I am speaking was described by Hegel[16] as an *Aufhebung*, a "sublation," a process of both annulling and preserving, of both passing-over and taking-up. In this process, what was evil, false, destructive, and oppressive in the past needs to be "refined away," to be allowed to die or to be put to death, while what was good, true, salvific, and liberating needs to be preserved and raised to new life in new forms. Perhaps the special responsibility of First World theology is to contribute all that it can to the revivifying side of the process, thus providing substance and resources for the new vision of humanity emerging from the Third World, from the underside of history—a side that must also become our side as we make the passage.

We must, however, avoid the illusion that this annulling and preserving can happen automatically or easily. In history there are always only partial victories of good over evil, and evil frequently prevails—if not forever, at least for long periods. In order for the process of sublation to work, *we* must help make it work, often at the cost of great sacrifice and suffering and with the tenaciousness of an almost defiant optimism.

We must have *the courage to think and to act*—to think with the utmost clarity about our situation, to act on the conviction that a new cultural paradigm, a new synthesis of values, can emerge in the postmodern age. By thinking that it *can* happen and by acting in accord with such conviction, we shall help *make* it happen.[17] The shape of the new paradigm is not yet clear in its details—it remains veiled in the mystery of temporal passage—but we have intimations of what it will be like. The stress will fall more upon the public than the private, the social than the individual, liberation than liberty, equality than hierarchy, inquiry than authority, praxis than theory, the ecumenical than the provincial, the plural than the monolithic, the global than the national, the ecological than the anthropological. These contrasts are often a matter of emphasis rather than of exclusion or simple opposition, but there is some variation between them in this regard: liberty, for example, is a value to be preserved, hierarchy a structure that needs to be replaced.

The new cultural paradigm calls for a new theological paradigm, a revisioning of the entire theological agenda, including questions of method, God, history, human being, ecclesiology, eschatology, and religious pluralism. Work on theological method must address both the cognitive questions raised by postmodernist criticism and the practical questions raised by liberation theology. In what sense can we actually *know* and *speak about* the realities affirmed by faith? To what extent does theology follow from praxis and become a form of praxis, a "reflective praxis"? A new theological anthropology must address the problem of the deep split between individual and social interpretations of human existence. We urgently need new models of the relationship of God and history that are noncoercive, nonsupernaturalistic, nonprogressivist, and nonlinear in their teleology—a post–salvation-history theology of history that can give a credible account of what it means to say that God "acts redemptively" in history. A new understanding of the relationship of Christianity to other religions will involve encounters and dialogue on the basis of equality and mutual transformations. Related to this is the recognition that Christianity is a global phenomenon and that it is being modified by other cultures as well as other religions.

The task of this book is to take up the agenda of a new ecclesiology, a new theology of the church—one that is nonhierarchical, nonprovincial, and nonprivatistic in its ecclesial vision, one that focuses upon the historicality as well as the spirituality of the church, recognizes its distinctive communal form, and thematizes its liberative praxis and ecumenical mission. This is my way of specifying the elements of the new paradigm as they relate to the ecclesial community; they will be elaborated in chapter 2. But our task is also to describe and evaluate critically the main features of classical ecclesiology, drawing upon resources from the Bible and theological tradition down to the Reformation, seeking out those elements of enduring value and truth that should be integrated into a new vision. This is the task of chapter 1. In chapter 3, I shall reflect briefly on the sort of ministry that would be appropriate to a theology of the church in the new paradigm.

Needless to say, ecclesiology cannot be pursued in isolation from the other elements of the new theological paradigm. Each of them has important implications for our topic. Questions of theological method will remain only implicit in this work, which I conceive as a kind of "reflective praxis," a thinking oriented to ecclesial praxis. I am assuming that human existence is shaped primarily in terms of social structures, yet I am also seeking a form of community in which free subjectivity is fulfilled. The issues with which a theology of history is concerned are fundamental to this project if we claim, as I do, that the ecclesial community is not merely a human product but the creative work of the Spirit of God. To claim this assumes a coherent way of understanding divine activity and presence in history—perhaps the most difficult theological question of our time. The context of religious pluralism has quite radical implications for the self-understanding of the Christian church, which can no longer credibly assert that outside itself there is no salvation. These and other issues are constantly present as we turn to our task, but for the most part they will be addressed only indirectly. Especially in times of transition, any theological project must remain incomplete and open-ended.

1

Elements of the
Church in the
Classic Paradigm

A revisioning of the church implies the existence of an earlier vision, or a plurality of such visions, that are not simply to be abandoned but are rather to be reconfigured in the light of new demands and expectations. Indeed, when critically refined, many elements of the classic ecclesial paradigm offer creative images and rich insights that will prove to be of value to our reconstructive efforts. In this chapter, I shall draw attention to several of these: the nature of the relationship between Jesus and the new community of faith; the meaning of the terms "ecclesia" and "church"; biblical images of the church (people, body, communion, Spirit); the "rule" or "realm" of God of which the church is a sign and sacrament; traditional marks or dimensions of the Catholic church (one, holy, catholic, apostolic); the Protestant distinction between the church visible and invisible; and the impulses toward both the church type and the sect type in the life of the ecclesial community.

1. CHRISTOLOGY AND ECCLESIOLOGY

Why and how did the historical figure of Jesus become a community-forming event? Why and how did a new religious community take shape in response to the life, ministry, and death of Jesus of Nazareth? These questions concerning the origin of Christianity are among the most complex and most elusive we face. They have been debated ever since the emergence of historical criticism, and I have no simple answers to them. At best I can offer some guidelines for reflection, distinguishing between historical and theological considerations.

21

Historical considerations. Both negative and positive historical evidence regarding the relationship of Jesus and the church may be adduced. On the negative side, it is clear in the first place that Jesus did not found a church. On literary, historical, and textual grounds, the evidence is unavoidable that Matt. 16:17–19 ("You are Peter, and on this rock I will build my church") is not a historical account but reflects the consciousness and interests of the Matthean community in its attempt to legitimate its Petrine leadership. Later the authority associated with Peter was extended to the Roman church by the story of Peter's going to Rome as its first bishop and being martyred there. Over against this attempt to establish a direct link between Jesus and the founding of the church, critical scholarship has shown that Jesus understood himself within the framework of Judaism and had no intention of establishing a "new" religion. Furthermore, even within the Jewish frame of reference, he never addressed himself to a select group separated from the mass of the people, a "holy remnant" of God's elect.[1]

It is clear in the second place that Jesus was not a cult hero. New religious sects often do in fact form about charismatic leaders, but this does not seem generally to have been the case with Hebraic religion. Abraham, Moses, David, and the prophets did not form sectarian movements. Such movements appeared in later Judaism, but their leadership was based on discipline and law rather than personal charisma, and in any event Jesus had no significant connection with them. He did not give a new law, did not claim authority on his own behalf, did not perform miracles in order to establish authoritarian claims, did not discipline dissidents. Though he does seem to have had a charismatic impact and attracted a wide following, he never called attention to himself or encouraged veneration of his person.

On the other hand—and here we come to the positive evidence —Jesus did proclaim the "nearness" of the realm of God, the *basileia tou theou*.[2] The image of the basileia was basically communal and social—an image of a new way of being human in the world in relation to God and neighbor that broke the "logic" of the old world, of ordinary human relationships. God's rule called forth a new human community, a communion of love, of liberation, of inclusion, of gratuity. The parables in particular evoked the vision of a "realm of freedom" and a radical alteration of conventional social and institutional structures. It is not surprising that in response to Jesus' proclamation, there should come into being a new kind of religious community, an "ecclesia of freedom" that in certain respects imaged and anticipated the basileia of freedom.

Moreover, Jesus gathered disciples who were to carry the word of the inbreaking basileia to the whole of Israel; he had a table fellowship with social outcasts (tax collectors, sinners, the sick and injured, women, Samaritans); he called for a "new and radical family"[3] based not on blood relationships but on human and ethical relationships (Mark 3:31–35: "Whoever does the will of God is my brother, and sister, and mother"); he challenged the authority of traditional religious and political leaders (Matt. 20:25–26: "You know that the rulers of the Gentiles lord it over them, and their great men exercise authority over them. It shall not be so among you"). These actions were a cipher or paradigm of a new quality of human and religious community; Jesus enacted what he proclaimed.

Theological considerations. The first point to be made is that the coming into existence of the church was a complex event happening over time. The "event of Christ," as John Knox puts it, includes "the personality, life and teaching of Jesus, the response of loyalty he awakened, his death, his resurrection, the receiving of the Spirit, the faith with which the Spirit was received, the coming into being of the church." The temporal duration of this event, Knox notes, "might be indefinitely extended" both forward and backward, and "a similar indeterminateness belongs to any historical event. . . . Events are the stuff of history; and history is a living, organic process, in which every part participates in the whole and the whole is present in every part."[4] On this view, it is a mistake to attempt to pinpoint the origin of the church or to think of Jesus as preceding the church as its founder. Jesus rather was part of the complex historical process of formation of what I shall call ecclesia, or ecclesial existence, ecclesial freedom, and ecclesial community (see sec. 2 below). Jesus was indispensable to the process but did not exhaust it. Theologically, we should have to say that what formed (and forms) ecclesial existence is the power or act or work of God.

What seems to have been definitive in the shaping of a new community of faith was the experience of the living presence of the risen Messiah. Jesus had not left his followers behind but was somehow "with" them. He was not with them in a visible, physical sense (the appearance stories in Luke and John make this clear), nor was it simply a matter of vivid recollections of him. Rather what

was with them was the "reality" he embodied—a divine-human
and an interhuman reality, a new way of being in the world whose
logic was liberating, self-giving love rather than hostility, alienation, a self-securing. The very reality or event of Jesus the Messiah
was with them, and this event was a community-forming event: he
was known, recognized, in the breaking of the bread (Luke 24:30–
31). The resurrection and the formation of the community are,
theologically speaking, one and the same event. The identity of
Christ is the identity of the community: this identity is no longer
that of a single individual but is now that of an ecclesial existence.
Christ is no longer he but has become we.

The functional genre of the primitive Christian community was
originally not Scripture or doctrine or cult but kerygma.[5] The
function of the kerygma was to witness to the Christ and to
announce to the world the redemption (the setting-free) accomplished in him. Later, of course, the community adopted a normative Scripture, it replaced kerygma by doctrine (which functioned
as law), and its celebration of Christ's presence took on cultic,
sacerdotal characteristics—which is simply to say that it took on
many of the features of religious communities in general. But
originally it was different. As a kerygmatic community, centered
upon the reality and presence of Christ, it was a nonprovincial,
nonexclusionary, nonhierarchical, noncultic community. The new
community of the Messiah was drawn from all nations to form not
a new nation but a universal community transcending all provincial
understandings of divine presence—whether localized in a people,
a land, a temple, a book, or a set of doctrines or laws. Its leadership
was charismatic and egalitarian rather than clerical and hierarchical. Its central act of community gathering was not cultic or
sacrificial, and it did not involve sacred objects; it was in fact a kind
of world-transforming praxis (Acts 2:45: ". . . they sold their pos-
sessions and goods and distributed them to all, as any had need").
Partly for these reasons, the community of the followers of Jesus
came to call itself an *ekklēsia* rather than a *synagōgē*.[6]

2. "ECCLESIA" AND "CHURCH"

In secular Greek, *ekklēsia* means simply "assembly." Etymologi-
cally, it suggests a summons or calling-out for the purpose of a
gathering, especially a political assembly. Some interpreters have
attempted to derive a theological meaning of the term from this
etymology, arguing that "ecclesia" designates the "group of men

called out of the world" by God.[7] Clearly, however, this is a spurious interpretation that goes against the sense of the term.

The word *ekklēsia* was commonly used by the Septuagint (the Greek version of the Hebrew Bible) to translate the Hebraic expression *qahal* or *qahal Yahweh,* "those called of God," "the people or congregation of God," "the people Israel." *Qahal* was sometimes, however, translated by a similar Greek term, *synagōgē,* literally "a gathering together," which in turn was the more common Septuagint rendering of *'edhah,* "those appointed (of God)." In Palestinian Judaism, *synagōgē* became the term commonly used to designate the Jewish religion and specifically its place of worship, the synagogue; thus the word took on distinctly cultic overtones. In Hellenistic Judaism, however, the term *ekklēsia* was used to designate assemblies of both political and cultic character. Under the conditions of Diaspora, these assemblies ensured for Jews their political as well as religious identity: the assemblies gathered both to praise God and to regulate the affairs of the community.[8]

Why did the primitive Christian movement come to identify itself as an ecclesia rather than as a synagogue? A plausible hypothesis is that after Jesus' death, a new community began to form when Palestinian Jews within the synagogue came, for whatever reasons, to believe that Jesus was the expected Messiah of Judaism. Those who believed this also began to include outsiders, non-Jews—Samaritans initially, then Gentiles, all those willing to say that their Messiah or Savior was Jesus of Nazareth. The practice of inclusion, together with the gradual elimination of Jewish customs and the seemingly blasphemous claim that Jesus was the Messiah of God, led to the Jewish Christians' becoming personae non gratae in the Jewish community, and they were eventually expelled from the synagogue, forced to become a new community outside Judaism (although still deeply attached to its institutions) and to find a place of gathering outside the synagogue.[9]

Originally the new community was nameless, but within a few years it had established its identity not simply as a network of *ekklēsiai* (assemblies) but as the *ekklēsia tou theou* (ecclesia of God) gathered in the name of Jesus Christ (see 1 Thess. 2:14). Surely both the Septuagint and the current Jewish Hellenistic usage were in the background. Like the Diaspora Jews, the early Christians gathered for purposes of worship as well as shared meals and community regulation. But this assembly was also believed to be the new *qahal Yahweh,* the new people of God, the new Israel. To articulate why this should be the case, and why the image of assembling, of "gathering into community," was so intrinsically appropriate for the new movement of Jesus-followers as to become its very *name* —to articulate this, a fleshing out of the image of "ecclesia" was required that went well beyond anything found in contemporary Judaism, the Septuagint, or secular Greek usage. This was accomplished by a rich profusion of metaphors, found especially in Paul and in the deutero-Pauline and early catholic epistles but also in the Gospels and Acts.

The term *ekklēsia* itself occurs primarily in the Pauline epistles and in Acts. There are three occurrences in Romans, sixteen in 1 Corinthians, five in 2 Corinthians, two or three each in Galatians, Philippians, and 1 and 2 Thessalonians—and another five in Ephesians, which reflects a post-Pauline christological perspective. In the authentic Pauline writings, the expression "the ecclesia of God" or "the ecclesia of Christ" is almost a formula and is filled with meaning only through the metaphorical associations that we shall discuss shortly. Eighteen occurrences are found in Acts, where it has a simply factual connotation referring to particular churches and reflects an already established usage, but the term is not found in Luke or any other Gospel except Matthew, where the two references (16:18; 18:17) are the product of later tradition, not actual words of Jesus, who obviously did not use the word *ekklēsia*, although he employed metaphors later taken to refer to the community of his disciples. Though not used in the Gospel of John, *ekklēsia* occurs six times in Revelation as a factual reference (e.g., "the church in Ephesus"). It is found only twice in Hebrews and, surprisingly, is hardly used at all in the so-called catholic epistles. For the most part, then, *ekklēsia* is in the New Testament a technical term, the standard designation of the Christian movement, referring either to the movement as a whole or to its local assemblies, and requiring theological elaboration through other terms.[10]

Latin had no separate term for the Christian community but simply borrowed and transliterated Greek *ekklēsia*, which was thus taken over by the Latin West and the Romance languages (*église* in French, *iglesia* in Spanish); *ecclesia catholica* became the recognized name of the Christian religion in the West.

In the Germanic languages, *ekklēsia* was translated by words that came from a different root: German *Kirche*, Swedish *Kyrke*, English "church." Luther thought that the root was *curia*, the Latin term for a political district, meeting place, or council; and thus in his view it was discredited through its association with the Curia Romana, the papal court. Consequently he avoided the term *Kirche* and preferred *Gemeinde,* "community" or "congregation." But more recent etymological studies have shown that the likely origin was the Byzantine popular form *kurikē,* "(house) of the Lord," which was brought into the Germanic languages by Arian missionaries. This in turn derived from the Greek adjective *kuriakos,* "the Lord's," "belonging to the Lord"—an adjective found in the New Testament, where it is not, however, applied to the ecclesia.[11]

The word "church" is laden with a host of historical and institutional associations. It is of course a perfectly good term and is simply the normal English translation of the Greek and Latin "ecclesia," although it lacks the suggestive etymological associations of the latter term. It is also possible, however, to adopt "ecclesia" into English, and there are certain advantages in doing so. It is then possible to use "ecclesia" (and related expressions, such as "ecclesial community," "ecclesial freedom," and "ecclesial existence") to refer to the *ideal, distinctive,* or *essential* features of the Christian church, those features which set it apart from other religious communities as a unique form of redemptive existence. Often these distinctive features are obscured in the actual historical manifestations of Christianity, although the ecclesia "exists" only in such manifestations. "Church," or better, "churches," can then be used to refer to the empirical, historical, institutional reality.[12] I propose to follow this distinction but not rigidly. "Ecclesia" and "ecclesial" as I use them will always carry the ideal or essential connotation, but "church" will sometimes be used in an encompassing sense, including both the ideal and the real, as in the expression "a theology of the church in the new paradigm." Thus in some contexts the contrast between "ecclesia" and "church" is intended while in others it is not. As to the appropriateness of even speaking of an "ecclesial essence," this is a matter to be discussed in some detail below.

Two other English words might be considered appropriate translations of *ekklēsia:* "congregation" and "community." The first comes closest to the actual etymological sense of the Greek, since it means to "gather together," but it is generally used to refer to local "congregations" rather than the whole church or the concept of the church. "Community" has the root sense of "building for mutual service," hence a "sharing," a "mutual participation," an "upbuilding through love." As we have seen, Luther used the German equivalent of "community," *Gemeinde,* as his preferred term for church, but the English word has secular as well as religious connotations. Nevertheless, it comes close to capturing the central meaning of *ekklēsia,* and I shall often employ it, especially with adjectival modifiers, as in "ecclesial community."

3. IMAGES OF ECCLESIA: PEOPLE, BODY, COMMUNION, SPIRIT

The community of believers in Jesus Christ did not attempt to form a cultic title from the name Jesus, and only later did they come to be known as Christians (the term *christianoi* occurs only three times in the New Testament and was first commonly used by Ignatius and pagan authors).[13] Rather, as we have seen, the preferred term of self-designation was "ecclesia," taken over with its Greek, Septuagint, and Hellenistic Jewish connotations but functioning as a formal term that required theological elaboration. This elaboration was provided by a profusion of metaphors and images from ordinary language and everyday experience. The metaphorical process that began with the parables and sayings of Jesus continued to characterize the way that believers thought and talked about God, redemption, the Messiah, and themselves; in a profound sense, Christianity was and remains a language-event.

The virtue of Paul Minear's book *Images of the Church in the New Testament*[14] is that it shows this profusion in all its diversity and lack of systematization. Minear identifies ninety-six images or analogies (e.g., "fish and fish net," "the boat," "the ark," "unleavened bread," "wine," "branches of the vine," "vineyard," "the fig tree," "God's planting," "building on the rock"). The disadvantage of remaining simply at this presystematic level is that it is mindboggling. In fact it can be argued—and Minear agrees—that *four* dominant images of ecclesia emerge from the diversity of New Testament literature and continue to reverberate through subsequent expressions of Christian faith down to the present day. My thesis is that the images work cumulatively, constituting a progressively more precise and theologically nuanced definition of "ecclesia." The four are "the people of God," "the body of Christ," "the communion (or fellowship) of faith, hope, and love," and "the creation of the Spirit" (or "the spiritual community"). To these four a fifth can be added, which is not strictly speaking an image of the church but is rather the telos, the eschatological fulfillment, of the church, *of which* the church is itself an image or sign: "the kingdom of God."[15]

People of God (laos theou). The image of the people of God is the earliest and most inclusive. Widely distributed in the New Testament, except for the Johannine writings, it marks Christianity's continuity with Israel. Israel thought of itself as a people in two senses: as a gathering or assembling for cultic and community purposes (Heb. *qahal* = Gk. *ekklēsia*), and as a nation in both a political and an ethnic sense (Heb. *am* = Gk. *laos*). The use of the image *laos theou* indicates that the ecclesial community was seeking to identify itself as a new Israel, a new people, in the second sense as well as the first. The image carried with it national, ethnic, and political connotations that were not lost but, rather, modified. Paul broadened the image to universal dimensions without losing sight of the fact that it specifies a temporal, historical, political reality. He applied to the church of Gentiles as well as Jews the words of Yahweh originally spoken in Hosea to Israel: "Those who were not my people I will call My People, and the unloved nation I will call My Beloved. For in the very place where they were told 'you are no people of mine,' they shall be called Sons of the living God" (Rom. 9:25–26 NEB). A people without national boundaries, a common language, or a single ethnic identity is a peculiar sort of people. It is an ecclesia.

Probably in light of its Hebraic ethnic associations, the image faded from prominence after Christianity became a largely gentile phenomenon. Echoes of it were heard in the apostolic fathers (Clement of Rome, Justin Martyr, Irenaeus),[16] and Augustine revived it in a new, nonprovincial form: the *civitas Dei*. It has been rediscovered in twentieth-century ecclesiology as a result of the impact of biblical studies and a recognition of the close connection between Israel and the church. Liberation theology has been attracted to the political dimension of the image, and as we shall see, it has played a central role in the black church, which senses an affinity with the oppressed people of Israel, a chosen people despite their suffering.

Body of Christ (sōma tou Christou). The second image, that of the body of Christ, helps to specify what is distinctive about the first: the *new* people of God is the body of Christ. This image is predominantly Pauline but echoes elsewhere in the New Testament as well. Part of Paul's genius was to seize upon a Hellenistic, organic image and to transform it in the direction of the Hebraic roots of ecclesial faith, at the same time allowing these roots to grow beyond their original cultural matrix. "Body," *sōma,* is both an organic and an ethical, social metaphor for Paul. It appears to have three levels of meaning when referring to the "body of Christ."[17]

1. Self-sacrifice for others: *the crucified Christ.* The most literal reference is to the physical body of the crucified Jesus. The eucharistic words of institution lie at the root of the metaphor: "This is my body, which is for you" (1 Cor. 11:24). But already a significantly new meaning has been introduced, one not ordinarily associated with bodies. Here the body becomes a symbol of self-denial, self-divestment, rather than of self-fulfillment and gratification.

2. Constitution of a new people, a social nexus in which self-giving love forms the bond of union: *the risen Christ.* Paul passes from the first meaning to the second in a single passage: "The bread which we break, is it not a participation [*koinōnia*] in the body of Christ? Because there is one loaf, we who are many are one body, for we all partake of the same loaf" (1 Cor. 10:16-17). It is not as though the ecclesia were a literal extension of the incarnation. It is rather that the self-giving love of Christ—his "body," given for us—now defines the unique intersubjectivity of the community of faith; he lives on in it and is corporately embodied by it to the extent that it actualizes the sacrificial quality of his life.[18] Thus the body image served as a framework for Paul's theology of the risen Christ (1 Corinthians 15). It also proved to be an exceptionally fruitful way to think about unity and diversity in the church and to keep the ecclesial vision continuously before his congregations (1 Corinthians 12—14).

3. Constitution of a new humanity: *the cosmic Christ.* In the deutero-Pauline epistles, Colossians and Ephesians, the attention shifts from the meaning of the presence of Christ in a local congregation to that of his presence in the whole cosmos. Here Hellenistic Jewish wisdom imagery has been appropriated: the world, having been created through Christ, is metaphorically his body and is to be reunited with its spiritual head by his resurrection. But the Pauline emphasis on the cross is also incorporated, and Christ is understood to permeate the world not in mystical or Stoic fashion but in the apostolic mission to which the ecclesia contributes.

Unlike "the people of God," "the body of Christ" has played a major role in the history of ecclesiology, especially at its second and third levels of meaning.[19] The idea of "the mystical body of Christ" first appeared in Cyril of Jerusalem and Cyril of Alexandria in the fourth century. "Mystical" derives from the Greek *mueomai,* "to be initiated into the mysteries," and the reference is to the initiatory ceremonies by which a person becomes a member of the church. These ceremonies include instruction, renunciation of evil, confession of faith, immersion in water, sealing with the Holy Spirit, and receiving the body of Christ in the Eucharist. Through this process an ontological participation in the very being of Christ comes about, a participation that is salvific or deifying.

The ontological identity of Christ and the church suggested by the image of "the mystical body" was pressed further by Augustine, who said that Scripture speaks of the one Christ with three points of reference: as the eternal Word equal to the Father; as the mediator between God and humanity; and as the church. "The head of the church is Christ, and the church is the body of Christ" (*Hom. on 1 John* 6.10). But also, "Head and body are one Christ: not because he is not whole without the body, but because he has also deigned to be whole with us, who even without us is whole and entire" (*Serm.* 341.9). Augustine was aware that this was not a simple identity, since he also spoke of the church as a *corpus permixtum,* a "mixed body," including both saints and sinners. He explained this possibility by introducing the distinction between the visible and the invisible church—the latter consisting of those predestined to salvation from before their creation.

Under the influence of Augustine, traditional Catholic ecclesiology came to distinguish three aspects of the one mystical body of Christ—the incarnate body, the eucharistic body, and the body that is the church—each being subsumed by the next. This formed the basis of the high ecclesiology of the Middle Ages. But a distinction that began to emerge in certain medieval theologians (Alexander of Hales, Albertus Magnus, Thomas Aquinas) between the mystical body and the church formed a basis for later criticism. Wycliffe identified the mystical body exclusively with the invisible church of the elect, as distinguished from the church of "prelates and priests." Calvin introduced another kind of distinction: according to him, the visible as well as the invisible church is the body of Christ, but this body is to be distinguished from Christ, who is its "head," its sole and sovereign head, displacing all earthly heads. The head rules the body but is not touched by the disease—the sin and weakness—that infects the body. (As in the case of the earthly

Lord, so also here the ordinary laws of physiology appear to be suspended.)

Communion of faith, hope, and love (koinōnia). The question becomes what *characterizes* the body of Christ that is the new people of God if, on the basis of what we have just seen, it is construed neither physically nor metaphysically but rather socially and ethically. What sort of body is it? This brings us to the third image: the body of Christ is in essence a new sort of communion or fellowship,[20] in which each individual finds identity and fulfillment through the others, a communion in which subjectivity is actualized in the form of intersubjectivity. In this way the distinctive love symbolized by Christ's own broken body is reenacted in the communal fabric of the church.

The New Testament literature uses the term *koinōnia* to name this reality. *Koinōnia* is referred to as one of the four fundamental practices of the primitive ecclesia by Acts 2:42, the others being teaching, the breaking of bread, and prayers. Although we are accustomed to speaking of the church as a "fellowship of faith," this may be a somewhat misleading expression taken alone and is found only once in the New Testament (Philem. 6). We hear more commonly of the *koinōnia* "of the Son" (1 Cor. 1:9; 1 John 1:3, 6), "of the blood of Christ" (1 Cor. 10:16), "of the Spirit" (2 Cor. 13:14; Phil. 2:1), and "in the gospel" (Phil. 1:5). In 1 Cor. 1:9, Paul writes, "God is faithful, by whom you were called [*eklēthetē*] into the fellowship [*koinōnia*] of his Son, Jesus Christ our Lord." It is not our faith that constitutes koinonia but the reverse, in the sense that koinonia is the matrix in which faith occurs—the koinonia of Christ, based on the faithfulness *of God.* Individual acts of faith do not together constitute a communion; rather the condition for the emergence of faith is the new possibility of communal praxis represented by the koinonia.

Thus the ecclesia is a communion or fellowship of faith because it is a communion of love, based on God's faithful love in Christ. It is in fact a koinonia of faith, hope, and love (1 Cor. 13:13), with these three "gifts" defining one another (although love is the "greatest," says Paul). These images reverberate throughout the tradition.[21] Augustine in particular developed the theme of a fellowship of love, whereas among certain scholastic and reforming theologians (notably Thomas Aquinas, Ockham, Luther), it was common to speak of the church as a fellowship of faith (*congregatio fidelium*). This was said specifically to counter the idea of the church's consisting principally of the clergy or of its being a hierarchical institution. The sense in which the church is a fellowship of hope is related to the image of the transformative basileia, to be considered shortly.

Creation of the Spirit (pneuma). If we ask what constitutes the koinonia, we are brought to the fourth of our images, that of the creative or community-constituting work of the Spirit. "Spirit," *pneuma,* is among the most elusive of categories for divinity, described biblically in terms of its constitutive function vis-à-vis the people of Israel and the ecclesial community. "Spirit" refers to that modality of divine activity whereby God indwells and empowers not merely human subjectivity but *inter*subjectivity. If the koinonia embodies the distinctive love of Christ and in that sense is related to Christ, whose presence it mediates, it derives from the creative work of the Spirit and in that sense is the "communion of the Holy Spirit," *koinōnia tou hagiou pneumatos* (2 Cor. 13:14; cf. Phil. 2:1). The themes of *ekklēsia* and *pneuma,* of community and Spirit, were woven tightly together by Paul and primitive Christianity, although there are no exact verbal correspondences.

To articulate this connection, Paul and his followers introduced a series of remarkable images of building. What the Spirit does is build, upbuild, create a community, an ecclesia. Our words "communion" and "community" derive from the Latin verb *munio,* meaning "build" or "fortify": a community is a mutual building, a building for service *(munus),* an upbuilding through love. The ecclesia is described variously as the "temple of God," *naos theou* (1 Cor. 3:16); a "spiritual house," *oikos pneumatikos* (1 Peter 2:5); the "household of God," *oikeioi tou theou* (Eph. 2:19); the "dwelling place of God in the Spirit," *katoikētērion tou theou en pneumati* (Eph. 2:22). The reference to the ecclesia as a "house" or "household" surely reflects the fact that Christians first gathered in house churches throughout the Hellenistic world.

"Building" is to be taken in both its verbal and its substantive sense; it is both a process and a structure, both an activity of upbuilding, calling, summoning, assembling, and the building, the assembly, the corporate entity that results from the process. The same may be said of "ecclesia," and we can now see why this term lends itself so well to a theological elaboration of what is distinctive about the Christian understanding of redemption: redemption entails precisely the process of the *formation of community,* and it is *actualized* in the community thus formed, a liberated, reconciled communion of free people.

Ephesians 2:12–22 contains a rich store of ecclesial images. The author, who may be assumed to stand in the Pauline tradition, begins by suggesting that the division of Jews and Gentiles into alien communities has been overcome "in the blood of Christ." Christ's purpose was to "reconcile us both to God *in one body* [*en heni sōmati*] through the cross, thereby bringing the hostility to an end." This "one body" is described in terms of the building images to which we have referred, and the "one Spirit" of God is active in the building process: "You are no longer strangers and sojourners, but you are *fellow citizens* [*sumpolitai*] with the saints and members of the *household of God, built* upon the foundation of the apostles and prophets, Christ Jesus himself being the chief cornerstone, in whom the whole structure is joined together and grows into a holy *temple* in the Lord, in whom you also are built into it for a *dwelling place of God in the Spirit.*" If Christ is the foundation stone, the artisan or builder is "God in the Spirit," and the edifice is the ecclesia in which the "dividing wall of hostility" has broken down and a single new humanity (*hena kainon anthrōpon*) is in the process of being fashioned.

In this way all the ecclesial images we have discussed are gathered up and modified. This new *people* of God is not to exist at enmity with the old; both peoples are to be incorporated into a single *body,* founded on the flesh and blood of Christ. This body is a true *communion,* in which there are no longer aliens and strangers but fellow citizens, members of God's household. And the bond or matrix of this building, household, temple, is the redemptive presence, the indwelling, the upbuilding, creative work of God as *Spirit.* Ecclesia, in brief, is the *community of the Spirit,* the *spiritual community;* and "God in the Spirit" is "God existing as community."[22]

In the doctrinal tradition,[23] Augustine was the first to expand upon this image in a profound way. The Holy Spirit is the bond of love and as such is the "soul" that indwells and quickens the mystical body, which is a fellowship of love. Thus Augustine combined our second, third, and fourth images. The idea of the Spirit as the "soul" of the body that is the church was employed by Thomas Aquinas in his attempt to moderate the ecclesiology of papal primacy.[24] The image was put to similar use by the Tübingen school in nineteenth-century Catholicism (J. A. Möhler, J. S. Drey) and by the French *nouvelle théologie* in the twentieth century (Emile Mersch, Henri de Lubac, Yves Congar). This was the background of the innovative ecclesiology of the Second Vatican Council (the "Dogmatic Constitution on the Church," *Lumen Gentium*), of which Hans Küng is one of the best contemporary representatives.[25] In Protestant theology, Paul Tillich's category of spiritual community reveals the theological potential of the image.

4. ECCLESIA AND BASILEIA

There is another biblical image to which the ecclesial community is related, that of the *basileia tou theou,* the "kingdom of God," "realm of God," or "rule of God."[26] The relationship here is quite different, however, from the ones we have just been considering. Not an image *of* ecclesia, the basileia is imaged *by* ecclesia: the ecclesial community is the spiritual-historical sign, sacrament, and foretaste of a transcendent, divinely given transfigurative ideal. As such, ecclesia and basileia can be neither identified nor dissociated.[27] Their relationship is "dialectical." It is misleading, however, to think of the relationship primarily in chronological terms, emphasizing the "eschatological" character of the basileia in such a way as to represent it as a future state of affairs—a future, whether near or distant, brought about by a supernatural act of God that brings history to its completion. Under the impact of the rediscovery of biblical eschatology, much of contemporary theology has taken this approach. But there are two fundamental difficulties: the approach perpetuates the myth of salvation history, and it makes Jesus' proclamation of the basileia into more or less propositional information about an external (chronologically future) state of affairs.

If we think of the kingdom of God as the final event, the telos of a history of salvation, then present, actual history will have one of three sorts of relationship to it. Special events or institutions in actual history will be identified with it, such as the hierarchical and imperial church; or history as a whole will be viewed as moving progressively toward its telos, whether religious or secular; or actual history will be viewed as irredeemably lost and evil, and there will be the expectation that it will be abruptly and cataclysmically terminated. All three of these views—the institutionalist, the progressivist, and the apocalyptic—are illusory. One of the marks of the new paradigm is that we know this to be the case. We know that absolutistic institutional claims of any sort are idolatrous. We know that, though history changes constantly, it does not seem to be advancing along a teleological line toward a progressively realized goal. We know that there is no credible evidence for a divinely wrought imminent and cataclysmic end. (*We* may bring history to an end in a nuclear holocaust, but to baptize that God's apocalypse is blasphemous—as well as extremely dangerous, since it could serve to legitimate nuclear conflict.)

Jesus' proclamation of the basileia is not a propositional but an "interactive" use of language.[28] It does not convey information about the future but challenges the normative values of society and entails commitments from its hearers in such a way that the proclamation already establishes and constitutes a new community. The basileia evokes a vision of a radical transformation or reversal of values, standards, and orders of life: not the power of money but the power of poverty, not the power of lordship but the power to serve, not the first but the last, not blood relationships but social and ethical relationships, not the logic of reward and punishment, domination and sovereignty, but the logic of grace, liberation, and love.

The question is how this vision of the basileia is related to the ecclesial community—how it is related so that the community is an anticipatory sign and sacrament of a new reality for which the community "hopes" but which it embodies always only partially. Here I shall just sketch a proposal that will be elaborated more fully when the first of the issues on the agenda of a theology of the church in the new paradigm is addressed.[29] The basileia is a principle or ideal that constantly challenges and transforms human relationships and historical circumstances. It is not a trans- or post-historical but an intrahistorical principle, never identifiable with actual states of affairs but standing over against them critically, constructively, productively. It is a *practical* principle or ideal, a principle of praxis, which is, however, actualized in concrete historical situations, struggles, and institutions only fragmentarily and ambiguously. It has and is the power of an ideal, a productive ideal, a lure, a paradigm. As such, it is the power that makes the church ecclesial and not simply a social gathering or club. But it transcends the ecclesial community, because it is the principle of the world as a whole, and it does not entail explicit recognition or confession of Jesus as the Christ. Jesus proclaimed the basileia as God's realm, not his own. But in the ecclesia the proclaimer has become the proclaimed. The ecclesia, I have said, is that people which understands itself as the body of Christ, a koinonia of faith, hope, and love, upbuilt by the Spirit of God, which is known also as the Spirit of Christ. In the ecclesia the basileia assumes the form of the community that is the body of Christ and the work of the Spirit—the "spiritual community." But the basileia takes on other forms as well and is at work outside and beyond the community of believers. Because ecclesia exists only in the actual historical manifestations of Christianity—there is no ecclesia apart from church—it is not a pure practical ideal like the basileia but is "mixed," is ideal-real, and thus can actualize only fragmentarily the saving, liberating power that it images or envisions unambiguously. God's rule is whole and true, the historical churches are fragmentary and ambiguous, and the ecclesial "essence" (as I shall call it) participates in both.

5. MARKS OF THE CHURCH: ONE, HOLY, CATHOLIC, APOSTOLIC

The biblical images we have been considering will be of value as we attempt to revision the nature of the church under the new paradigm, in chapter 2 and the Epilogue. They did not, however, play a central role in doctrinal reflection on the nature of the church, which emerged only gradually. Theological treatises on the church began to appear only in the late Middle Ages, at a time when the church itself had become a subject of controversy.[30] The closest approximation to a widely accepted credal formulation is the statement introduced into the Constantinopolitan supplement to the Nicene Creed in 381: "We believe in one, holy, catholic, and apostolic church."[31] Subsequently, the qualities of unity, holiness, catholicity, and apostolicity came to be considered marks of the true church, although what each of the qualities actually consists in has been a subject of continued debate.

Two sorts of questions immediately present themselves. First, are these four credal attributes *really* the marks or signs by which the true church, the ecclesial community, may be recognized? In postmedieval and post-Reformation theology, they became increasingly the marks of distinction of the *Roman* Catholic church, to be used apologetically against other branches of the church—first the Eastern Orthodox church, and then, especially, the Protestant churches. As we shall see, the Reformers did not deny these attributes, but for them other matters were more decisive, namely, the pure teaching of the gospel and the proper administration of the sacraments.

Second, have these marks or attributes ever actually been *realized?* Is not the church in fact often the very opposite of what it claims to be, or at the very least are not these marks actualized only paradoxically and ambiguously? Is it not self-evident, today as always, that the Christian church has been not only united but divided; not only catholic (in the double sense of universal and orthodox) but also partisan, particular, and in continual need of renewal; not only holy but also profane and sinful; not only in possession of apostolic authority but also committed to serve the world and enhance human freedom? The answer to these questions can only be yes. They underscore the relativity and historicality of the church, and the issues raised here will be considered further in relation to the impact of historical consciousness and the other transformations engendered by the new paradigm.

But first it will be helpful to get the classic formulation of the doctrine of the church into view, and I therefore propose to consider briefly each of the four marks, taking them up in slightly different order from that of the credal formula. I certainly am not attempting a full-scale analysis of Catholic ecclesiology but am continuing to search out retrievable elements from the tradition which can serve as foundations of a new ecclesiology.[32]

Unity. Although Pauline theology located the principle of ecclesial unity in Christ, or in the body of Christ, the third-century bishop Cyprian, who established the main lineaments of a Latin ecclesiology that prevailed for over a thousand years, relocated it to the episcopacy. "You ought to know," he wrote in opposition to the Novatian schismatics, "that the bishop is in the church, and the church in the bishop; and if any one be not with the bishop, that he is not in the church. . . . The church, which is catholic and one, is not cut or divided but is indeed connected and bound together by the cement of bishops who cohere with one another" *(Ep.* 68.8).[33]

In saying this, Cyprian was simply reflecting a well-established practical arrangement that arose in a time when transportation and communication were extremely difficult. The bishop was the pastor responsible for all the parishes within a fairly small geographical region. He traveled about to these parishes and linked them together by his persona. Communication between geographical regions was possible only through a network of bishops, who were

in communication with one another in the form of written corre-
spondence and who occasionally came together for meetings, or
councils. That is why the bishops, and especially the collegium of
bishops, became the symbol of the unity of the church. Only later
did the bishop of Rome rise to a position of primacy, appropriating
to himself the claim to be the basis and center of the church's
unity.[34]

The question for us is how the mark of unity can be sustained in a
time when it can no longer be claimed that the church "is not cut or
divided." How are we to deal with the historical fact of schism and
division in the church, as well as with the existential fact of
diversity and plurality in all human activities? We wonder, furthermore, if the basis of unity can be merely juridical (whether
episcopal, papal, presbyterial, confederate, or whatever) rather
than spiritual. Augustine, for example, argued against the schismatics of his time, the Donatists, that it is *love* which demands unity
and nonseparation—the love that is poured out by the Holy Spirit
and is the very soul of the church. Love can be sundered and still
unite, and hence there was a reluctance on Augustine's part to
conclude that the Donatists were in no sense in the church.[35]

The exigency for unity does not reside in scriptural or doctrinal
proofs or in particular historical practices but in the fundamental
logic of Christian faith, which is oriented to a single central figure
and event—God's redemptive action in Christ—and which is
intrinsically nonprovincial in character, with no divisions or exclusions legitimated on the basis of race, nationality, location, sex,
creed, language, or the like. In view of this exigency, the burden of
proof must rest on those who contend that a given state of
circumstances demands division, schism, or separation.

The precondition of unity is the recognition of and tolerance for
diversity, plurality, difference. Unity does not reduce diversity but
rather allows it. Those who cannot tolerate difference (of creed,
interpretation, practice, structure) are those who insist on separation in order to preserve a rigid identity. In this sense, unity is very
much like the love of which Augustine spoke, and love is indeed the
true basis of unity. Unity allows for diversity and difference, but
not division and separation. These matters will be discussed further
in chapter 2.

Catholicity. Ignatius of Antioch early in the second century was the
first to speak of a "catholic church," meaning the whole or

complete church in contrast to the local episcopal churches. The Greek adjective *katholikos* (from *holos*, "whole," "entire," "complete") has this precise sense. The adverbial form occurs once in the New Testament (Acts 4:18), but not in reference to the church. The original and literal meaning of "catholic" as "whole" and "universal" was gradually inflated, however, in response to various challenges and movements, to include the senses of (*a*) orthodoxy, that is, the true, nonheretical, nonschismatic church (doctrinal catholicity), (*b*) extension over the whole earth (geographical catholicity), (*c*) a church larger in numbers than any other (numerical catholicity), and (*d*) a church older than all others (temporal catholicity).[36]

Vincent of Lérins expressed these several senses in a famous formula ("that which is believed everywhere and always by all"), but it was Augustine who gave the notion of the *ecclesia catholica* —the only lawful religion of the Roman Empire after the edict of Theodosius in 380—its full theological elaboration. The adjective was no longer a description but part of a proper name, the name of the universally accepted, official, consummate religion of the civilized world. He frequently described this church as "mother" ("You are safe who have God for your father and his church as your mother"), and he was so convinced of its inner vital power and the truthfulness of its message that he could say that he believed in the gospel only on the authority of the Catholic church. The sense of participation in a reality that is vital, powerful, ancient, holy, and true has always been part of the appeal of Catholicism.

Küng suggests that if we wish to get behind the name to the adjective in its original signification of "whole" and "universal," we could substitute for "catholic" the word "ecumenical," meaning "the whole inhabited earth." " 'Ecumenical' and 'catholic' are words that are closely linked not only in their original meanings but also in their Christian usage."[37] Küng also suggests that if we mean by "catholic" the "whole," "complete," or "universal" church, this should be construed not in the sense of spatial, temporal, or numerical extension but rather in the sense of "identity" (or "inner wholeness," as Jürgen Moltmann says).[38] In this respect, of course, catholicity can and should be claimed by Protestants as well as Catholics, but with the understanding that such identity is maintained only through a continual process of reformation. The truly "catholic" church is also the truly "reformed" church.

Holiness. The tension between the church's essential being as the body of Christ or spiritual community and its actual historical existence as a sinful, fallible people was emphasized by a succession of rigorist, spiritualist sects. The first of these, the Montanists (mid-2d cent.), claimed to be inspired by the Holy Spirit, allowed no forgiveness of postbaptismal sin, practiced an ascetic discipline, and welcomed martyrdom. Tertullian accepted certain of the Montanist practices, including the role of inspired prophets, and defined the church as a society of the Spirit whose true members are spiritual persons or "saints." Hippolytus went further, describing the church as the "holy society of those who live in righteousness," which must exclude sinners. A similar ecclesiology was championed by the Novatianists in the third century and by the Donatists in the fourth.

In response to such pressures, a distinction gradually developed between the true, spiritual, or heavenly church and the empirical, historical church, which contained error and sin. Under Neoplatonic influence, Clement of Alexandria and Origen understood the heavenly church to be both preexistent and eschatological, the ideal toward which the earthly institution was oriented and for which it was to prepare its members. Neither of them would have accepted the later distinction between the "invisible" church, containing only the elect, and a "visible" church, also including condemned sinners, since they were universalists who believed that all persons finally would be saved and that the empirical church would be subsumed in the spiritual. The invisible-visible distinction first appeared in Augustine under the impact of his predestinarian doctrine. In his view the invisible, true, or holy church comprises the fixed number of saints predestined before the foundation of the world, known only to God. Although the distinction proved useful in later ecclesiology, Augustine's version of it was unnecessarily harsh, probably because of his long conflict with the Donatists and Pelagians.[39]

A richer, more balanced theological elaboration of the holiness of the church was found in Thomas Aquinas's *Exposition on the Apostles' Creed.* "The church is holy," he wrote, "by the indwelling of the blessed Trinity." In this *Exposition,* he described the church, in the words of Congar, as a "living body compacted out of a plurality of members, all quickened and governed by a single living principle . . . or soul," which is the Holy Spirit (more precisely, the Trinity indwelling as Spirit). Congar points out that the description of the Spirit as the soul quickening the body of humanity was not just a pious metaphor but a powerful technical factor in Aquinas's theology, since in his view "only a 'dynamic' principle genuinely divine can direct and move [humanity] toward the objects of the divine life." God as Spirit is the "dynamic power of the [ecclesial] life of humanity moving Godwards." Congar rightly adds, "Herein St. Thomas sees the first and deepest notion that can be had of the Church."[40]

Among the leading theologians there was no simple divinization or sacralization of the empirical church. The holiness of the church was conceived to derive solely from God's presence in it—God's spiritual and sacramental presence—but this presence was never thought of as something the church can appropriate as its own or claim credit for. The sanctity and efficacy of the sacraments were seen to be independent of the worthiness of priests and people. Against the sectarian purists, it was recognized that the distinction between holiness and sinfulness runs *through* the church rather than dividing the holy church from the profane world. Luther's *simul justus et peccator* (at once justified and sinful) applies not only to individual believers but to the church, which is not only the *communio sanctorum* (communion of saints) but also the *communio peccatorum* (communion of sinners).[41] In worship the church is taken up into the life of God, but central to the same worship is the confession of sin and the recognition that everything is dependent upon divine grace and forgiveness. The problem *we* have is not in acknowledging the church's sinfulness and profanity but in knowing how it can be appropriately described as "holy."

Apostolicity. An "apostle" literally is one who is "sent forth." According to tradition, the apostles possessed an original and unique authority in virtue of having been commissioned and sent forth by Jesus for missionary preaching, and having witnessed the risen Lord. They were messengers, witnesses, authorized representatives. But whether they were authorized by Jesus himself is a debatable question. Paul included among the category of apostle some who had not known Jesus according to the flesh, such as Barnabas and himself. But later tradition limited the category to the Twelve (and possibly Paul), who were given special status and authority vis-à-vis all other disciples and believers. The term "apostolic" came to mean "having a direct link with the apostles of Christ."[42]

The notion of apostolicity became dangerous when it entered into a literalized myth according to which there is a direct, demonstrable, empirical link between the original apostles and successive generations of ecclesiastical leadership, whose claims to authority are thereby legitimated. In fact, the myth of apostolic succession (first mentioned by Clement of Rome) has served as the legitimation of a particular form of polity, namely, one that is sacerdotal, episcopal, hierarchical, and exclusively male. By its very nature this polity has vested authority in a group of specially sanctioned individuals, and its tendency has been to become increasingly monarchical and absolutistic. Obviously it was necessary for the postapostolic church to adopt some form of definite institutional structure, including an ordered and recognized ministry, and it was probably inevitable that this structure should reflect the patterns of religious and political authority characteristic of Hellenistic and Roman culture. The charismatic forms of ministry present in the apostolic church were lost, and a juridical model of reality was adopted with its accompanying system of rewards and punishments. What is regrettable is not so much that this happened but that the hierarchical, absolutistic, and juridical forms were regarded as divinely sanctioned and eternally legitimated, so that the church was unable to change when new political possibilities and expectations opened up in the modern and postmodern periods. The Protestant churches have proved nearly as rigid in their polity as the Catholic, and differences in polity more than any other single factor have stood in the way of the ecumenical movement.

Is it not possible that the mark of apostolicity, differently construed, could guard against such developments and such rigidity? The significance of apostolicity would seem to be that it requires that matters relating to the institution, organization, ministry, and offices of the church be treated *not* in terms of given dominant patterns of religious and political authority and social organization but rather always with reference to the founding event of ecclesia, the paradigmatic figure Jesus of Nazareth, to whom the apostles witnessed and whose gospel they proclaimed. Although the original apostolic witness cannot be repeated (and in this sense there are no successors to the apostles, no "apostolic succession"), the apostolic *mission* can be handed on, and this is a mission of service in obedience to the Lord.[43] Such service ought to be liberating rather than authoritarian, collegial rather than hierarchical, inclusive rather than exclusive, suffering rather than triumphalistic, a ministry of the Spirit rather than of the letter. Apostolicity seems to mean that the ministry of Jesus remains a paradigm for subsequent ministries, although this cannot be a matter of simple imitation or repetition. A possible model for ministry in the new paradigm will be considered in chapter 3.

6. THE PROTESTANT PRINCIPLE: THE CHURCH VISIBLE AND INVISIBLE

The fundamental issue at stake in the Protestant Reformation was not that of justification, grace, sacraments, or Scripture, but the question of the nature of the church.[44] It is true that the historical, political, economic, cultural, and religious influences bearing on the Reformation were exceedingly complex. It is also true that the immediate instigating factor was the attempt to rectify specific abuses in a decadent Renaissance Catholicism. It is true, finally, that Luther's personal starting point was not the question of the church as such but the question of salvation: how can one be certain of salvation in light of the perversity and pervasiveness of sin and the evident futility of good works to set one right before God? But Luther's discovery of the answer in the Pauline theology of justification by faith led to a new understanding of the church and a demand for radical reform of the whole of church life in accord with the gospel. Although Luther did not intend this reform to lead to schism, the issues were so deep, so complex, and so extensive in their implications, that in a historical sense one can say that division in the Western church had become inevitable. It was not the result merely of excesses on the Reformers' side and of obstinacy on the Catholic side but of historical forces that were reshaping Europe. The Reformation released creative new energies, produced genuine reform, and played an instrumental role in the emergence of modern consciousness, but the consequences of the division of Christendom were also profoundly negative, since the division left a legacy of conflict, rivalry, continued splintering, and loss of religious credibility which encouraged the growth of secularism.[45]

One result is that it is not possible to speak of a single Protestant ecclesiology, since Protestantism itself soon divided into numerous movements, each with distinctive ecclesial features: Lutheran, Calvinist, Anabaptist and Baptist, Anglican, Methodist, Congregational, Evangelical, as well as literally dozens of other rival sects that have continued to proliferate to this day.[46] It is possible, nonetheless, to identify certain distinctive features that represent what is decisively new and theologically significant in Protestant ecclesiology. In so doing, one is forced to overlook many historical differences and to focus primarily on the great Reformers themselves.[47]

Luther and Calvin did not deny the classic marks of the church but added others which they thought were necessary to define the true church in the polemical situation of their time, namely, the pure preaching of the gospel and the right administration of the sacraments of Baptism and the Lord's Supper. Luther subsequently expanded the list to seven "signs," including not only the preaching of the Word of God, Baptism, and the Lord's Supper (the "primary signs") but also (as "secondary signs") the power of the keys (i.e., the power to judge and forgive sin), ministry (the office empowered to exercise the first four signs), public prayer, and Christian life shaped by the cross. These were signs of the "visible church" by means of which the presence of the "invisible church" in it could be measured and tested.

What appears to have been truly distinctive about the Reformers' ecclesiology was the way they adopted and transformed the Augustinian distinction between the invisible and the visible church. Recall that in Augustine's view the invisible, true, or holy church comprises the fixed number of saints elected before the foundation of the world, known only to God; this invisible church is "mixed in" with the visible church, which includes also sinners, those who are not among the elect. On this view, the invisible church seems to have a metaphysical status as a suprahistorical realm of spiritual beings or saints. Luther in particular rejected this metaphysical realism, moving instead in the direction of understanding the invisible church as a *critical theological principle* that permitted quite radical criticism of the church's institutions, dogmas, and practices. Calvin, in adopting and even extending Augustine's predestinarianism, also subtly modified the distinction. For him, "invisible" and "visible" do not refer to two churches or realms but refer to two ways of speaking about the one church. This one church—visible yet invisible—is the body of which Christ is the sole head and principle.

Luther's discussion of this matter is more helpful for our purposes than Calvin's. In his treatise *On the Papacy in Rome* (1520),[48] Luther says that Scripture speaks of Christendom in only one way, as a "community" or "assembly" of "all those who live in true faith, hope, and love": "As we pray in the [Apostles'] Creed, 'I believe in the Holy Spirit, the communion of saints.'"[49] This community is hidden, transcends specific geographical loci, and is an object of faith rather than perception; its members (who are not fixed in advance) are known to God alone. The other, human way to speak of the church is to call it "an assembly in a house, or in a parish, a bishopric, an archbishopric, or a papacy." Luther says he will call these two churches by two distinct names. "The first, which is natural, basic, essential, and true, we shall call 'spiritual, internal Christendom.' The second, which is man-made and external, we shall call 'physical, external Christendom.'" These two churches cannot be separated, but they must be distinguished. On the basis of the distinction, Luther uses the "first Christendom" as a critical principle to test the validity of the second—in this case, the papacy in Rome. Later in his career, he came to recognize more clearly the necessity of historical, institutional embodiments of the spiritual, essential church, and for this reason he enumerated the visible signs of a true church. But he never ceased using the distinction as a basis for theological criticism.

The invisible church, then, encompasses an *essential meaning and power* of ecclesia that functions both *critically* and *productively* vis-à-vis all historical forms of the church. That this is what was implicit in the ecclesiology of the Reformers, especially Luther, was first brought out by the nineteenth-century historical theologian Ferdinand Christian Baur, who attempted to articulate the distinctive "principles" of Catholicism and Protestantism. The "idea of the church," according to Baur, is the "essence of Christianity" itself, namely, the "unity and union of God and humanity . . . in the person of Christ" or the "idea of reconciliation." Now, in Catholicism this ecclesial "idea" had become completely *identified* with its concrete historical manifestations in the form of the official dogmas of the church and its episcopal-hierarchical structure. By contrast, the tendency in Protestantism had been "to retract the idea from the reality of the visible church and to *separate* idea and manifestation to the full extent of their distinction." Both of these are extremes, according to Baur. The true Protestant insight is that the relation between idea and manifestation, or between the invisible and the visible church, is a *dialectical-critical* one: the two churches are to be neither separated nor identified but understood to exist in a tensive relationship with each other. There can be no ecclesial essence apart from its actual historical forms—the idea of the church is no Platonic ideal—but the historical churches can never be regarded as wholly adequate embodiments of the essential truth of reconciliation. Thus all forms of ecclesiastical absolutism must give way to the freedom of the subject, the independence of the state vis-à-vis the church, and the principle of historical relativity. Baur called this dialectical-critical view the Protestant principle, suggesting that its full implications were not worked out until the Enlightenment of the eighteenth century. The critical principle implicit in the Reformation was not extended to the whole structure of church dogma or to the theology of the church itself for another two or three centuries.[50]

This interpretation of the visible-invisible distinction in Protestant thought will be of direct assistance as we address one of the issues of the new paradigm—an issue inherited, to be sure, from the first Enlightenment—namely, how the relationship of "spirituality" and "historicality" is properly to be understood in the church. For reasons that will become clear, I prefer the expression "ecclesial essence" to Baur's "idea of the church." I shall also be guided by Tillich's appropriation and development of the idea of the "Protestant principle" in a well-known essay of that title, where he defines it as the "protest against any absolute claim made for a relative reality, even if this claim is made by a Protestant church. ... It is the guardian against the attempts of the finite and conditioned to usurp the place of the unconditional in thinking and acting. It is the prophetic judgment against religious pride, ecclesiastical arrogance, and secular self-sufficiency and their destructive consequences."[51] The symbol of this principle is for Tillich the cross—a symbol that negates itself as it points beyond itself. Tillich here formulates the principle primarily in negative terms, as a *critical* principle, by which the empirical churches are tested and judged. In addition, I wish to stress, as indeed Luther and Baur recognized, that the principle is also positive: it is a *productive* principle or paradigm by which the empirical churches are empowered to be truly ecclesial. Tillich attends to this aspect more clearly in later writings.[52]

7. CHURCH AND SECT

Another sort of distinction has been introduced into the discussion of ecclesiology by Ernst Troeltsch, namely, the distinction between "church type" and "sect type."[53] Both types, according to Troeltsch,

> are based upon fundamental impulses of the gospel. The gospel contains the idea of an objective possession of salvation in the knowledge and revelation of God, and in developing this idea it becomes the church. It contains, however, also the idea of an

absolute personal religion and of an absolute personal fellowship, and in following out this idea it becomes a sect. The teaching of Jesus, which cherishes the expectation of the end of the age and the coming of the kingdom of God, which gathers into one body all who are resolute in their determination to confess Christ before humanity and to leave the world to its fate, tends to develop the sect type. The apostolic faith, which looks back to a miracle of redemption and to the person of Jesus, and which lives in the powers of its heavenly Lord—this faith, which leans upon something achieved and objective, in which it unites the faithful and allows them to rest, tends to develop the church type. Thus the New Testament helps to develop both the church and the sect.[54]

Although it has often been in the sects, according to Troeltsch, that "the essential elements of the gospel [were] fully expressed," the mainstream of Christian development has followed the church type, since it was able to come to terms with the world and to exercise influence upon public institutions through a necessary process of "compromise" rather than withdrawing from the world into independent, private sanctuaries. During the early centuries there was in fact a good deal of fluctuation within the church between the two types; it was only with the full development of the church type in the late medieval sacramental-hierarchical institution that sects began to appear as independent countermovements (e.g., the Waldensians, Wycliffites, and Hussites). Up to the beginning of the eighteenth century, the sects remained thoroughly suppressed, even within Protestantism (e.g., the Anabaptists, Mennonites, Millenarians, and Quakers). But since then the situation, according to Troeltsch, has reversed: the church type has been in retreat and the sect type on the rise, "until today the latter has issued in a pure and radical individualism." Through pietism and romanticism, the sect type entered into the theological and cultural mainstream. The individualization and privatization of religion mean that a concept of the church is no longer necessary; the watchword of today is, "Religion is a private matter."[55]

Troeltsch viewed this as part of the cultural crisis of the early twentieth century, and he called for a retrieval of a concept of the church that would provide the foundation for an authentic understanding of religious community and public responsibility. What must be given up in the church type is everything that associates the church with a hierarchical, sacerdotal, "miracle-channeling," triumphalistic institution.[56]

From Troeltsch's analysis we may conclude that both the church type and the sect type are subject to characteristic perversions—the church type to institutionalism, the sect type to individualism and privatism. Individualism and privatism are the predominant perversion of modernity, although the effects of institutionalism are still very much felt—no longer so much in the form of suprahistorical claims as historicized in bureaucracies and managerialism. As we take up the challenge of a theology of the church in the new paradigm, these perversions will be very much in mind.

2

Toward a Theology
of the Church
in the New Paradigm

The Enlightenment and post-Enlightenment period (the so-called modern era) posed the second major crisis in the history of the Western church. The first was the Reformation, which challenged the unity, holiness, and apostolicity of the Roman Catholic church. The Enlightenment challenged the supernatural, suprahistorical character of the church left largely intact by the Reformers, thus radicalizing and extending the critical principle of the Reformation itself. Enlightenment and post-Enlightenment theology articulated the relativity and historicality of the church, associating it with human quests for freedom and community while attempting to defend and transform the church concept in the face of sectarianism, individualism, secularism, and thoroughgoing rationalism. The first major ecclesial issue of our time is one bequeathed to us by the Enlightenment, namely, how in light of the church's historicality and relativity we can understand it as a "spiritual community." This question has by no means been resolved by modern theology, although significant contributions have been made. The problem has only become more severe under the impact of postmodernist criticism, with its questioning of the meaningfulness of any historical construction and any transcendent reference.

In the latter part of the twentieth century we seem to be entering upon a second Enlightenment, a new watershed, a new cultural and theological paradigm shattering the monolithic character and hegemony of the Western church as a whole, which has been predominantly Euro-American, white, male, and bourgeois. Precisely this crisis is the condition of possibility for a rebirth of the ecclesial

51

community, a rebirth from below and from outside the established structures—*ecclesiogenesis* as Leonardo Boff calls it.[1] Black religion in America, the liberation theologies of the Third World, and European political theology have set forth a new vision of ecclesia as pluralistic, emancipatory, prophetic, and transformative, while feminist theology has unmasked and challenged the church's massive sexism and patriarchalism. The ecumenical movement has made us aware that Christianity is a global religion, while the encounter with other religions is deepening our awareness of the relativity of Christian faith and of the need, for the sake of human survival, of entering into genuinely reciprocal and mutually transformative dialogue with other religions.

I am led in this fashion to three sets of issues that set the agenda for a theology of the church in the new paradigm: these concern (*a*) the relationship of spirituality and historicality in the church, (*b*) the church and the praxis of liberation, and (*c*) ecumenism, world Christianity, and encounter among the religions.

1. THE SPIRITUALITY AND HISTORICALITY OF THE CHURCH

Ecclesial Essence

The Enlightenment forced theology to thematize the historicality of the church as never before, recognizing the institution to be finite, fallible, and relative and to share many of the characteristics of social groups in general. At the same time, no viable ecclesiology can surrender the conviction that the church is the continuous creative and redemptive work of God, who indwells and empowers it as Holy Spirit. The question is how the church can be both a divine gift and a human activity, both a spirit-filled community and a historical institution, without there being an identity of these dimensions of its being but without there being a separation of them either.

As we have seen, this is the way Baur posed the question in his reformulation of the traditional distinction between the invisible and visible church. He recognized that the question had taken on new urgency with the emergence of historical-critical consciousness, which made it impossible to think of God's providential or redemptive action as a miraculous, suprahistorical disruption of the historical nexus. This action would rather show itself in terms of a distinctive shaping or configuring of the historical process itself. The historical process is "empowered" or "shaped" by something ideal or essential that is distinct from the process itself but is not separable from it. "Essence" does not have the metaphysical status of a separated supernatural realm or power, nor is it a projection of ideal attributes; rather it is precisely the *essence* of what *exists*, of what is *real*, historically real. Unlike the Platonic ideas, it is "ideal-real," containing within itself the relationship to the real; it is a fundamentally *historical* category, a category of historical interpretation.[2]

What is the "essence" of the church, and how is this "ecclesial essence" related to "ecclesial reality"? The formal answer is that the essence is constituted by the spiritual community, the redemptive community shaped and empowered by—in some sense identical with—the indwelling of the Spirit of God, and that this essence is ambiguously and fragmentarily embodied in the empirically existing churches. But how is such an answer to be unpacked and elucidated? That, in one form or another, has been the central question of critical Protestant ecclesiology since the early nineteenth century, and it has also been taken up in a variety of ways by post-Enlightenment Catholic theology. In order to engage the question, we shall begin with Schleiermacher and Hegel, two thinkers who were of definitive importance for the whole subsequent development. We shall then turn to Troeltsch, a seminal and prophetic figure whose work at the beginning of this century has until recently been neglected. Finally H. Richard Niebuhr and Tillich, two more recent theologians who have made important contributions to our subject, will be considered, though many others could as easily be discussed.[3] My own proposal will be presented as a modification and further elaboration of Tillich's views, incorporating insights from the others as well.

Schleiermacher. A new understanding of the church emerged in Enlightenment historiography—notably that of J. L. Mosheim and J. S. Semler—which viewed history in a pragmatic, functionalist, nonsupernaturalist way, distinguished between true religion ("spiritual, moral, free") and church doctrine, construed the church as an association on a par with other human societies such as the state, and stressed the principle of individuality and subjectivity.[4] But the first great post-Enlightenment ecclesiology was formulated by Schleiermacher, who sought to avoid the reductionist tendencies of rationalism while incorporating rationalism's essential gains. Under the influence of romanticism, he had already in his *Speeches on Religion to Its Cultured Despisers* (1799) stressed the essentially social and communal nature of true religion. But it was in *The Christian Faith* (1821; 1830)[5] that he systematically worked out a new concept of the church. Defining the church as the "fellowship of believers," which has a central place in the "constitution of the world in relation to redemption" (§ 113), he located the origin of the church both in divine election (here he shared the Augustinian-Calvinist outlook) and in the "communication of the Holy Spirit." It is in developing the latter theme that Schleiermacher's own theological genius is most evident. He defines the Holy Spirit as the "common Spirit of the new corporate life founded by Christ" (§ 121) or, more fully, as the "union of the divine essence and human nature in the form of the common Spirit animating the life in common of believers" (§ 123). The Holy Spirit is a "specific divine efficaciousness working in believers"—a *common* Spirit, not a "person-forming union," as in the case of the two natures in Christ (§§ 123–25). What Schleiermacher is attempting here is an understanding of how the church is founded upon a divine reality working nonsupernaturalistically in the constitution of a human fellowship characterized by redemptive love. The union of the divine and the human in the church is analogous to that in Christ yet with a difference, since in the one it occurs individually and in the other only communally (see § 122). Moreover, it is in and through the ecclesial community that the "redemption accomplished by Jesus of Nazareth" (§ 11) is made efficacious for believers of all ages and communicated to the whole world.

Hegel. Starting from quite different philosophical premises, Hegel arrived at a similar and equally seminal concept of the church, in the final part of his *Lectures on the Philosophy of Religion* (1821–31).[6] Hegel clearly recognized the essential place of the cult in religion: it gives expression to the "practical" form of the religious relationship, representing the moment of concrete communion with deity and divine self-reconciliation. For the Christian religion, cultic praxis takes the form of the "community of the Spirit," which originates with the transition from the sensible presence of God in Christ to God's spiritual presence in the community of faith. The essence of this community is a unique, transfigured intersubjectivity, distinguishable from all other forms of human love and friendship. Privatistic and exclusivistic modes of existence are set aside, as are distinctions based on mastery, power, position, sex, and wealth; and in their place are actualized a truly universal justice and freedom. The name Holy Spirit signifies the unifying and liberating power of the "infinite love that arises from infinite anguish," the same love that was objectively represented on the cross of Christ but that now works inwardly, subjectively, building up a new human community: "This is the Spirit of God, or God as the present, actual Spirit, God dwelling in his community." Thus "the community itself *is* the existing Spirit, the Spirit in its existence, God existing as community." Like Schleiermacher, Hegel is positing an identity between the Spirit of God and the "common Spirit" of the ecclesial community. God in the modality of Spirit *is* the redemptive, transfigurative power that indwells and constitutes a new human intersubjectivity, an intersubjectivity shaped by the paradigmatic love of Christ, which is an "infinite love in infinite anguish."

This community, which has the status of ideality or essentiality, *realizes* itself. "The real community is generally what we call the *church*"—with its doctrinal, sacramental, devotional, and institutional forms. Furthermore, the "spirituality of the community" is realized in "universal actuality," in the course of which the community itself is "transformed." "Universal actuality" means the ethical, political, and intellectual forms of the secular world. In the "ethical realm" (family, civil society, state), "the principle of freedom has penetrated into the worldly realm itself," and the latter "is freedom that has become concrete and will that is rational." In other words, the reconciling, liberating love that is the essence of the spiritual community must be actualized not only in the individual heart and in the institutional church but also in the world in the form of rational freedom. Hegel's final view of the matter appears to be that the community of the Spirit should not remain simply ecclesiastical; rather it is to become a historical community in the world.

Troeltsch. Our expression "ecclesial essence" is very similar to what Troeltsch called the "essence of Christianity." In a classic essay on this concept,[7] Troeltsch says that "essence" is the "abstraction peculiar to history":

> Large coherent complexes of historical events are the development of an idea, a value, or a line of thought or purpose, which gradually develops in detail and consequences, which assimilates and subordinates alien materials and which continually struggles against aberra-

tions from its leading purpose and against contradictory principles threatening from without.

Essence thus understood is both a *critical* principle and a *developmental* principle. On the one hand, it is used to evaluate and judge critically all historical expressions of the "driving force" of an idea or value. On the other hand, it is an "entity with an inner, living flexibility, and a productive power for new creation and assimilation," a "developing spiritual principle, a 'germinative principle' as Caird calls it, a historical idea in Ranke's sense, that is to say, not a metaphysical or dogmatic idea, but a driving spiritual force which contains within itself purposes and values." As such, an essence "shapes" or "configures" new ethical and cultural "syntheses"; it is the power of historical creativity and novelty.[8]

Obviously the essence of Christianity cannot be identified with the institutional church. Nor, according to Troeltsch, can it be identified with a normative theological concept such as the idea of incarnation or of divine-human reconciliation (along the lines of the Hegelian school, Baur in particular), nor even with the idea of the kingdom of God as proclaimed by Jesus (Adolf von Harnack, Albrecht Ritschl). The essence is not a simple concept such as "the fatherhood of God," "the infinite value of the human soul," "the higher righteousness and the commandment of love" (Harnack's famous formulation). It can only be a "complex idea which determines the specifically Christian form of the basic ideas of God, world, human being, and salvation which are linked together in all religion." The closest Troeltsch comes to an actual formulation of the essence of Christianity is to say that it "contains a polarity within itself" and is like an ellipse with two focal points. "Christianity is an ethic of redemption whose world-view combines optimism and pessimism, transcendence and immanence, an abrupt polarization of the world and God and the inward linking of these two."[9] Christianity both radically criticizes the world and radically transforms it; it is at once eschatological and ethical. Later I shall argue that this tension characterizes the essence of ecclesia, which mediates, so to speak, between the pure basileia vision of Jesus and the actual existence of the churches in the world. What is the source and foundation of this essence, an essence that has redemptive, transformative power in personal and historical life? Troeltsch is always reluctant to speak facilely about God. But it is clear that, in his view and as a personal confession, what shapes and transfigures human existence ecclesially is the "divine ground of life," the "divine Spirit" ever pressing the finite toward a hidden final goal.[10]

Niebuhr. H. Richard Niebuhr was deeply influenced by Troeltsch in many ways. In a brief attempt at a "definition of the church" in *The Purpose of the Church and Its Ministry* (1956),[11] Niebuhr took the Troeltschian "polarity" and applied it with fresh insight. "The author of this essay," he writes, "must employ the method of polar analysis; that is, he must try to do justice to the dynamic character of that social reality, the church, by defining certain poles between which it moves or which it represents." The essential reality of the church, the ecclesial community, cannot be reduced to any one of these poles but rather occurs in the dynamic movement between them. The first and the last of the polarities identified by Niebuhr are not polarities within the church but ones in which it participates as itself a kind of pole. These are, in the first place, the polarity between the divine "object"—the rule or realm of God, or simply God—and the human, historical "subject," the church. "Negatively, the church is not the rule or realm of God; positively, there is no apprehension of the kingdom except in the church; conversely, where there is apprehension of, and participation in, this Object there the church exists."

The second of the external polarities is that between church and world. The world is not the object of the church, as God is; rather it is *"companion* of the church, a community something like itself with which it lives before God." The world also has a relation to God, since the salvation of the whole created order is the ultimate divine aim, but the world "knows" God only as the "unknown God" and hence rejects God or does not worship God. Thus the church has a mission of proclamation and healing to the world, but on the other hand, the world provides the larger matrix in which the church subsists, and sometimes it works in partnership with the church toward the end of increasing, if not the love of God, at least the love of neighbor.

The other polarities identified by Niebuhr are all *internal* to the structure of the church, namely, the polarities of community and institution, unity and plurality, locality and universality, and Protestant and Catholic. We must say that the church is "both-and," and hence it is intrinsically a "polar" or "paradoxical" reality. We can see that Niebuhr is taking some of the classic images and marks of the church and thinking about them dialectically. The spiritual essence of ecclesia does not reside on one side of these polarities but in the *dynamic movement between them.* It is precisely the empirical church's outward relationships to the divine object (its "holiness") and to the world (its "apostolicity") that keep it inwardly a dynamic, fluid reality, permitting it to be neither merely a spiritual community nor merely a social institution, neither merely a monolithic unity nor merely a splintering of rival groups, neither merely something present just here and there wherever two or three are gathered nor merely an abstract universal ideal, neither merely Protestant protest nor merely Catholic substance. The church is truly ecclesial only to the extent that it is all these things simultaneously, with its contrasting characteristics working in critical reciprocity.

Ecclesia is not a simple thing or entity but a complex relational nexus in its totality—the relationship of God (basileia) and church (ecclesia), of church and world, of community and institution, of unity and plurality, of locality and universality, of Protestant and Catholic. Because this is the sort of reality the church essentially is, we must constantly struggle against the temptation of "confusing proximate with ultimate goals." "Denominationalism not the denominations; ecclesiasticism not the church; Biblicism not the Bible; Christism not Jesus Christ; these represent the chief present perversions and confusions in church and theology." The ultimate goal of the church is simply "the increase among [people] of the love of God and neighbor."[12]

Tillich. An equally dialectical thinker, whose innovative approach to ecclesiology, in volume 3 of *Systematic Theology,*[13] differs from that of Niebuhr and Troeltsch, Tillich reflects a conceptual apparatus that is closer to Schleiermacher, Hegel, and German idealism, although he has also been deeply influenced by modern existentialism. In accord with the tradition, Tillich states that the church is both a spiritual reality (the "body of Christ," the "invisible" church) and a social group of individual Christians (the "visible" or empirical church). To designate the first element or aspect, he has appropriated the term "spiritual community" (he capitalizes it but does not indicate its intellectual heritage). The spiritual community is constituted by the "spiritual presence," which is simply the Spirit of God present in human spirit, the presence of the divine life within human life. Spiritual presence is the power of New Being, the power that creates unambiguous yet fragmentary life both in individuals and in the sociohistorical process. The expression "unambiguous yet fragmentary" means "appearing under the conditions of finitude but conquering both estrangement and ambiguity."

Tillich contends—and this is one of his most important contributions—that the category of spiritual community is neither realistic (a supernatural, heavenly realm of spiritual beings—as Augustine thought) nor idealistic (a construction of ideal attributes projected onto the screen of transcendence, which the empirical churches are supposed to approximate) but "essentialistic"—a "category pointing to the power of the essential behind and within the existential." Its ontological status is that of *power*—not causal power but creative and directive power. "The Spiritual Community does not exist as an entity beside the churches, but it is their Spiritual essence, effective in them through its power, its structure, and its fight against their ambiguities." It is the "inner *telos* of the churches, . . . the source of everything which makes them churches." But the spiritual community also extends beyond the churches: it is "latent" in social and religious groups other than the Christian churches as well as being "manifest" in the latter. By means of it, the three functions of human life—morality, culture, and religion—are united, no longer existing as separate realms. Viewed this broadly, it is difficult to distinguish the spiritual community from the other symbols of unambiguous life discussed by Tillich, namely, the kingdom of God and eternal life. In fact, he virtually identifies Spiritual Presence with the kingdom of God *within history,* simply stating that they draw upon different symbolic materials. This is one of the difficulties with Tillich's proposal.

The church is a "paradoxical" reality, according to Tillich: it participates both in the unambiguous life of the spiritual community and in the ambiguities of life in general and of religious life in particular. Its two aspects—one theological, the other sociological—should be neither *identified,* as in "official Roman Catholic doctrine," nor juxtaposed in unresolved *contradiction,* as in certain forms of Protestant ecclesiology. Rather they are related *paradoxically.* As an indication of the paradoxical character of the church, Tillich argues that the "marks" of the spiritual community—holiness, unity, universality, faith, and love (note that catholicity becomes universality, apostolicity is inexplicably dropped, and hope is reserved for part 5 of the system)—can be ascribed to the churches only by adding the qualifier "in spite of." The churches are holy in spite of their sinfulness, are essentially united in spite of their empirical divisions, are universal despite their particularity, are faithful despite their ambiguous religiosity, and are communities of love in spite of continuing estrangement.

Neither identification nor separation. What is the relationship of "ecclesial essence" or "spiritual community" to the basileia (the rule or realm of God) and to the historical, empirical churches? I wish to propose a set of relationships that involve distinction without separation or identification. In this, I shall be guided by the theologians whose views have just been summarized, as well as by the discussion in chapter 1 of "ecclesia and basileia" and the "Protestant principle."

The *basileia tou theou* is a metaphor or symbol of God's rule that utterly transforms, redeems, reconciles, and liberates historical existence and human relationships as a whole—a rule that constitutes the world as God's realm, a realm of freedom. It is a communal or social image, which envisions a communion of love, freedom, inclusion, equality, and gratuity. As such it is the telos of the world, but it is not to be thought of as being realized teleologically or progressively. It transcends history yet works within history as both a paradigm and a power.[14] As a paradigm, it offers a new shape, figure, or gestalt by which the world is reconfigured or transfigured. As a power, it is not causal but rather creative, directing, shaping, luring power. Thus, while it has the status of pure ideality over against empirical states of affairs, it is what I have called a *productive* ideal, a principle of *praxis,* or (borrowing an expression from Kant) a "pure practical ideal," an ideal that is intrinsically active or effective in the very articulation of it. The divine gestalt—the basileia gestalt—is the way God *acts* redemptively and efficaciously in the world. It lures, shapes, empowers, configures the world—the whole world, the world of nature as well as of the whole of history. It takes shape in a plurality of historical movements, groups, religions, cultures, works of art, and ethical and intellectual systems. It does so, of course, only fragmentarily and ambiguously, and for the most part anonymously and latently. But the basileia itself is nonfragmentary and unambiguous: God's rule as such is whole and true.

In the ecclesial or spiritual community, the basileia assumes a determinate religiohistorical form—the form of the Christian community of faith, the community that identifies itself as the new people of the God of Israel, the body of Christ, the koinonia of faith, hope, and love, the creation of the Spirit of God. Ecclesia is an image, sign, sacrament, and foretaste of the basileia, embodied in a diversity of historical churches. As such, it discloses the basileia vision unambiguously but actualizes it only fragmentarily. If what it images is the "realm of freedom," it is the "ecclesia of freedom." In it a new kind of corporate life is being shaped that is "free." It is free from not only sin and estrangement but all culturally specific conditions of redemption or provincial modes of existence, whether defined by nation, ethnic group, sex, class, language, law, tradition, or piety. In this new corporate life, we are free to be for and with the other and with the whole of humanity under God in a quite radical way, the full implications of which are still hidden from us.

In the fundamental distinction between God and history —between infinite and finite—ecclesia belongs on the side of history, finitude, and world; the basileia belongs on the side of God. But it is misleading to speak this way, for the distinction is not a simple one but dialectical. The God we know in faith is the God who is spiritually present in the world—not sensibly, perceptually, immediately present, but present through historical mediation —and the world we know in faith is a world that derives its "essence" from that which transcends the world. Thus we must insist that the ecclesial community is at once a spiritual and a historical, a "divine" and a "human" reality. It is at once the "existence" of God ("the Spirit in its existence, God existing as community") and the "essence" of the historical churches. Essence is a category that unifies the ideal and the real: it is the ideal manifested in the real (this is what "spirit" means), and the real raised to the ideal (the essence of what exists). As such, it is a category of both theological and historical interpretation. It is a theological category, because the essence of what exists is ultimately God (the ground or power of being, being itself); it is a historical category, because historical process is shaped and empowered by the interplay of the essential and the existential—an interplay the outcome of which remains always partial, incomplete, broken, and ambiguous.

Another way of making the same point is to say that the ecclesial community is a spiritual community. Spirit is a difficult concept that has often been criticized for being vague, vacuous, and dualistic (implying a contrast between the physical and the mental, the body and the soul, the natural and the human, the secular and the holy). I am using the term, however, not in that sense, which reflects the influence of Platonism, but rather in the sense employed by Hegel, which is closer to the meaning of the biblical terms for "spirit," *pneuma* (Greek), and *ruach* (Hebrew), both of which convey the image of blowing, wind, breath (breath of life). The same is true of the English word "spirit," which comes from the Latin *spirare,* "to blow," "to breathe." Spirit is what is alive, active, vital, moving; hence in ancient times it was frequently symbolized by fire—a material image of an immaterial vitality. Far from being dualistic, "spirit" is a *mediating* term: it is the ideal *manifested in the real,* the *unity* of idea and nature. Spirit is the ideal or the rational, not in and for itself but *embodied* in consciousness; hence there can never be spirit without nature, without embodiment. This is as true for God as for human being. God is Spirit insofar as God is present to, active in, and embodied by what is other than God, namely, the natural and human worlds.

Thus in the Bible "Spirit" refers to that modality of divine activity whereby God indwells and empowers the forces of nature, the people of Israel, the ecclesial community, and individual persons. Similarly, as we have seen, Hegel understands the "Spirit of God" to be "God as the present, actual Spirit, God dwelling in his community."[15] In another text Hegel says that "the spirituality of God is the lesson of Christianity": "Christian theology . . . conceives of God . . . as Spirit and contemplates this, not as something quiescent, something abiding in empty identicalness but as something which necessarily enters into the process of distinguishing itself from itself, of positing its other, and which comes to itself only through this other, and by positively overcoming it—not by abandoning it."[16] Thus, like "essence," "spirit" is a mediating term that unifies the ideal and the real; it is intrinsically ideal-real. The spiritual is the *unity* of the spiritual and the historical, it "overreaches" the spiritual and the natural.[17] As such, it seems to be a precisely appropriate term for designating the essential meaning of "ecclesia," and it should not have to be abandoned to Platonizing interpretations. Besides, it has the advantage of providing a gender-inclusive way of talking about God and humanity —indeed, of talking about them as interrelated not individually but corporately, in the "spiritual" community.

The spiritual community does not exist apart from the empirical churches. Its determinate, distinctive embodiment is in the historical Christian communities. I depart from Hegel's view that the spiritual community is to become a world-historical, secular, postecclesial community, and from Tillich's view that it extends beyond the churches, assuming other, latent forms as well. Both these views tend to confuse basileia and ecclesia, as well as church and world. To be sure, analogues of ecclesial existence are found outside the ecclesial community. The power of God's rule is at work throughout the world, shaping human existence in accord with the gestalt of the basileia, in a plurality of cultural, political, ethical, and religious traditions and forms. But I wish to reserve the word "ecclesial" for that community which explicitly recognizes and confesses the God of Israel and Jesus and which maintains an intentional link with the one believed to be the Christ, whose body the church is.

This is not to say that ecclesia is exhaustively realized in the churches; to the contrary, what it envisions unambiguously is actualized only fragmentarily and ambiguously in the churches. If we intend the term "church" to comprise *both* ecclesial essence and empirical churches, then we must insist, together with Tillich, Niebuhr, Troeltsch, and Baur, that it remains a thoroughly paradoxical, polar, dialectical, tensive reality.

The distinctions and connections I have attempted to establish between God and history, and between the key terms "basileia," "ecclesia," and "church," are set forth diagrammatically in the accompanying figure.

Basileia and Ecclesia

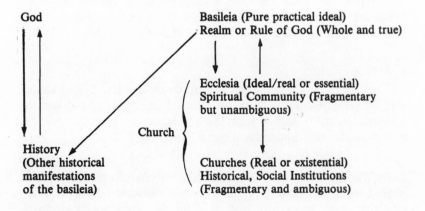

God

Basileia (Pure practical ideal)
Realm or Rule of God (Whole and true)

Ecclesia (Ideal/real or essential)
Spiritual Community (Fragmentary but unambiguous)

Church

History
(Other historical manifestations of the basileia)

Churches (Real or existential)
Historical, Social Institutions
(Fragmentary and ambiguous)

Ecclesial Sociality

The characteristic perversion of ecclesia in the post-Enlightenment period is that of individualism and privatism, which is one of the negative heritages of the sectarian tradition. In American Protestantism, which conforms in many respects to the sect type, this has often been combined with an uncritical acquiescence to the norms of popular culture. By privatizing religion and removing it from the public sphere, conservative and evangelical Protestantism has tended to destroy Christianity's critical, prophetic power, even if an orthodox belief system has been maintained. Liberal Protestantism, in maintaining a passion for social justice, has also tended to view religion as a matter of individual piety and humanistic ideals. The conservatives have lost *relevance,* the liberals have lost *transcendence;* hence both have capitulated to the demands of the culture and can readily subserve political, social, and economic interests.[18] Frequently the churches have functioned as nothing more than means of satisfying private therapeutic needs through counseling, ideology, and clublike activities. Questions of truth and redemptive community have been subordinated to those having to do with the successful adjustment of individuals to the exigencies of life. Ironically, this has occurred in a time when the social sciences have greatly enriched our understanding of the church as a social institution, of how every aspect of religious belief and practice serves social functions and can be understood in sociological terms. Individuals are socialized by religious groups —but in ways that reinforce the ideology of personal piety.

Two sorts of questions present themselves: (1) What common features do the churches have with other social institutions? (2) What are the (ideally) distinctive features of its sociality, features that contribute to the actualization of ecclesial essence?

Common Features

The first question is the subject of a vast literature, yet even a limited acquaintance with it (for which I am directly indebted to Howard Harrod) shows that the churches serve a number of common and well-understood social functions:[19]

Socialization. As agents of socialization, the church helps to pass on shared meanings from one generation to another—both its own traditions and the cultural values of the dominant social groups.

Each new generation must be socialized in the lore and values of those who have gone before.

Social control. Social control is an aspect of socialization. At one time the church controlled the dominant intellectual, political, and moral forces of society. This is no longer the case, but the regulation of certain values such as honesty, duty, patriotism, cleanliness, and helpfulness has been relegated to the churches, and this is often the hidden or indirect purpose of youth activities in particular.

Social cohesion. Integration into and acceptance of the system of values of the dominant culture can be promoted by the churches either positively or negatively. An example of the negative role of the churches can be found in the way they enable individuals to disburden themselves of alienating experiences and feelings.

Conferral of status. Human beings have a need for recognition, status, ranking. Lower-class and minority churches have often *conferred* status on deprived peoples; middle-class churches may *receive* status through association with wealthy and prominent communicants.

Social fellowship. Humans also have a need for fellowship, involving mutual recognition and intimacy among reasonably like-minded individuals.

Social philanthropy. One of the oldest social functions of the churches is philanthropy. It is also one of the easiest to promote, since, unlike the demand for justice, it generates little social conflict. It ignores the social systems that create the need for philanthropy and rather addresses concrete needs on a limited scale.

Social reform or transformation. The six functions we have just described are all maintenance functions. It may be necessary to maintain social stability, but if that is all the churches are able to do, they are not ecclesial communities. They are lacking the one thing needful, the transformative vision embedded in the biblical and theological tradition. The tradition contains an enormous potential for social transformation; the potential power of religious meanings and convictions is incalculable. But for the most part these resources remain untapped and well hidden. It must also be acknowledged that the effective application of these resources requires social and political skill.

Distinctive Features

The second question concerns the distinctive social features of the ecclesial community, features that are necessary for the community's survival and identity. Following a suggestion of Edward Farley, I shall distinguish here between the ecclesial community's distinctive temporality and its distinctive intersubjectivity.

Distinctive temporality. Every social institution perdures over time and must have means of maintaining its identity beyond a single generation, of sustaining its founding memories and normative traditions. James Gustafson addresses primarily this question in his book *Treasure in Earthen Vessels.*[20] The church, he says, is a community of language, of interpretation, of memory and understanding, and of belief and action. Through processes of communication, interpretation, understanding, reliving, and reenactment, the community maintains continuity with a unique center of meaning, the person-event Jesus Christ, which is rendered contemporary and efficacious through these processes. The processes have a double reference: to the objective representation of meaning in the documents, symbols, and rites of the community, and to the internalization of meaning by its individual members. A community, says Gustafson, is essentially a time-process: a community of memory and expectation, a community that has an "objective spirit" by means of which we are able to make the lived experience of the past our own lived experience, a community in which the past comes alive through the communication of significant symbols.[21]

As far as the ecclesial community is concerned, the institutionality required for temporal maintenance includes interpretive activities (proclamation, teaching of Scripture and tradition, interpretation of the present situation) and sacramental activities. The sacramental activities are means of bringing forth the past symbolically and relating the holy to various elements of ecclesial life.

Distinctive intersubjectivity. With distinctive intersubjectivity, our concern is with the spatial as opposed to the temporal dimension of a social structure. Farley argues in *Ecclesial Man*[22] that ecclesia is characterized by a "determinate intersubjectivity," a "specific structure of co-intentions which makes the faith-community distinctive as a community." "Intersubjectivity" designates that stratum of a social world which is pre-institutional and which is made up of a structure of intentionalities directed toward oneself and toward others (e.g., of intending oneself as husband and the other as wife, or vice versa). These co-intentionalities occur pre-reflectively and are the foundation for actual empirical relationships between persons and for specific institutional arrangements. They are at the core of what is distinctive about a determinate social world.

In the case of ecclesia what we find is a set of co-intentionalities engendered by the experience of redemption. Redemption from what? From idolatry and flight, which are illusory, alienating attempts at "self-securing" against the threat of existential chaos, which humanity must refuse if it is to be human but which it generally refuses only sinfully and disruptedly. Redemptive existence entails the co-intentionalities of freedom and obligation, which heal the disruptions of idolatry and flight by intending the other as oriented toward the transcendent rather than toward chaos or self. These co-intentionalities constitute the unique intersubjectivity of ecclesia, which has a peculiarly "self-surpassing" character: it knows no ethnic, spatial, or temporal boundaries and is intrinsically nonprovincial. There are no absolute strangers, for God's redemption has no specific cultural conditions; it is radically universal, available in and through any cultural wrappings. The wrappings do not disappear, but they are relativized. At this point, the distinctive intersubjectivity of ecclesia coincides with what I have called ecclesial essence, which is to say that this essence is a transfigured way of being communally human in the world and before God. Farley goes on to argue that the realities of faith—the transcendent God, the historical redeemer Jesus Christ, the cosmos perceived as creation rather than chaos —are apprehended as socially mediated in ecclesia; they are experienced along with the "essence" of ecclesial community. Ecclesial community is the epistemological foundation of faith's cognitive claims.

Finally, the institutional activity required to maintain this distinctive intersubjectivity is the activity of nurturing, caring, and justice—nurturing the formation and preservation of the community, caring for specific and individual human need, engaging in the praxis of social justice by means of which the community ministers to the ills of the world. The three institutional features I have mentioned—interpretation, sacramentality, and caring and justice—are the only ones that seem to be essential for the institutional embodiment of ecclesia's distinctive temporality and inter-subjectivity.[23] Beyond these exist a large number of institutional options, many of which may indeed contribute to the *bene esse* (well being) of the church but not to its *esse.*

2. THE CHURCH AND THE PRAXIS OF LIBERATION

If the ecclesial community is centrally concerned with the occurrence of redemption, and if redemption means being set free or released from a binding power, sin, or debt, then we can say with Hegel that Christianity is and has always been the "religion of freedom."[24] It was Paul more than anyone else who introduced the language of freedom as a means of interpreting the meaning of the Christ-event. He did so by appropriating the Greek term *eleutheria* and transfiguring its meaning.

For Paul, freedom has both a negative and a positive sense. Negatively, it means liberation from sin, law, death, and the worldly powers. This is the primary sense in which freedom is still understood by most Christians: it means salvation, my personal salvation, from sin, from my futile attempts to compensate for sin through obedience to the law, from bondage to physical existence, and from the cosmic and psychological powers that hold me in thrall. It means something like justification by grace through faith, and it was this dimension of the meaning of Christian freedom that was powerfully recovered by the Protestant Reformation.

But freedom also has a positive sense for Paul: it means not only being set free from "bondage to decay" but also obtaining the "glorious liberty of the children of God" (Rom. 8:21). Similar imagery, which associates freedom with a renewed relationship of human beings to the world and to God, occurs in Gal. 4:22–31, where Paul concludes that "we are not children of the slave but of the free woman"—that is, of Sarah, who symbolizes the true covenant and the new Jerusalem. Here freedom has become an end in itself: *"For freedom* Christ has set us free" (Gal. 5:1).

In this positive signification, Paul has taken over and transfigured conventional understandings of freedom. If in the Oriental world, only *one* was free—the monarch or ruler—for the Greeks and Romans, freedom entailed participation in a free *community:* the city-state or polis, the empire, the family and heirs of a free man. But in the Greek and Roman worlds, only *some* were free.[25] The very word *eleutheria* designated those who belonged to an ascendant group or were citizens of the polis, by contrast with oppressed subjects, slaves, children, and women. Citizenship rights were restricted to adult males, and the whole structure of Greek and Roman politics was based on the institution of slavery. It was the labor of slaves (debtors and foreigners taken captive in battle) that freed the *politēs* (citizens) from having to struggle for the necessities of life, enabling them to devote their activities to the truly human realm, the realm of freedom, of speech and action, the polis. Freedom meant self-determination (as distinct from being controlled by others or by the laws of nature) and membership in a privileged community.

But the free community of which Paul speaks—the new Jerusalem, the kingdom of God, the body of Christ, the ecclesia—is no longer privileged, restricted, alienated, provincial. It is not based on blood, sex, race, inheritance, or property. It is based rather on the conviction that all human beings are God's children—children of the one Lord who clears the earth of enthralling idols and sets God's people free. This community is built up by a distinctive kind of self-giving love in which the other is served for the sake of the other rather than for one's own sake—in a true *imitatio Christi*. In this community, "there is neither Jew nor Greek, there is neither slave nor free, there is neither male nor female; for you are all one in Christ Jesus" (Gal. 3:28). Thus Paul gives powerful expression to the new corporate consciousness that emerged in response to Jesus, who mediated God's redemption in a way that is intrinsically nonprovincial and radically universal. In the Christian world—in principle, at least—*all* are free.

The liberation movements have helped us to recover this second, positive sense of Christian freedom and to perceive implications of it for historical praxis which escaped Paul since he was thinking primarily in an eschatological context. Thus he did not directly attack the practice of slavery, the subordination of women, and the tyranny of the Roman Empire. These things, along with all other earthly power arrangements, were passing away and insignificant. Unfortunately they did not prove to be so. If redemption is to occur in human life, the Pauline eschatological vision must also become a historical vision. If we do not insist on this, it becomes easy, all too easy, for the church itself to slip back into the conventional human patterns of provincialism, patriarchy, exclusion, and exploitation, while paying lip service to freedom abstractly, negatively, and in purely religious terms. The liberation theologies have forced us to deprivatize Christian freedom and to recognize that it entails concrete historical, political, and social praxis. In light of the liberation theologies, we must insist that if there is a single essential quality of the church in the new paradigm which embraces all its other marks, it is that of freedom—ecclesial freedom. In what follows, I shall attempt to show how reflection and praxis from three of the main arenas of liberation theology are reshaping our vision of the church.

The Black Church

The black church is rooted in what Peter Paris calls the "black Christian tradition,"[26] a nonracist appropriation of the Christian faith which functions as a critical and prophetic principle within the black community and beyond it. The core of this tradition and its authoritative basis is the "biblical anthropology" that affirms the "freedom and equality of all persons under God." This, the very "essence of the Christian faith," was lost when the white churches of North America allowed themselves to become part of the ideological and social structure that legitimated the enslavement of black Africans in order to civilize the new world, and then continued to sanction segregation and racism after the abolition of slavery. It is precisely the black church that recovered the essence of ecclesia from this terrible distortion, and even today it can be said that the black church is the only truly nonracist church in North America.

How is it that the "religion of freedom" came to sanction and encourage a much more demonic form of slavery than anything found in the ancient world—demonic because practiced purely for purposes of obtaining a cheap labor supply and because justified by an ideology of racial inferiority?[27] A fifteenth-century papal bull permitted the enslavement of heathen Africans—but on the condition that the captives be set free upon their conversion to Christianity. This practice was followed in the American colonies but was increasingly opposed by slaveholders, until laws were enacted specifying that slaves would not become free by accepting Christian faith and baptism. Thus Christianity was deprived of its manumitting power. Arguments were developed to justify converting slaves without abandoning slavery. Slaves were converted to Christianity partly out of a guilty conscience on the part of slaveholders (at least the slaves' immortal salvation was assured), but also to wipe out surviving traces of African religion and to create a more docile, obedient servant class: slaves were taught that it was God's will that people of color should be enslaved and that the races should not mix, and they were assured that they would receive their reward in heaven.

One of the ironies of American history is that the slaves, indoctrinated in this alien religion of the masters, nevertheless discovered its true meaning—its liberative, redemptive essence —over against this emasculation. This happened in large part through what E. Franklin Frazier has called the "invisible institution"[28]—the underground "invisible church" of the slaves who gathered secretly to sing, pray, shout, preach, and read. The visible church of the slaves was of course under the supervision of their masters; here slaves were instructed in the Bible and exhorted to be obedient, to accept their servitude, and to acknowledge slavery as God's will. Independent services and Bible reading were discouraged or forbidden. Frederick Douglass pointed to the irony in the fact that Protestantism, the religion of the Word, refused to permit slaves to read the Word of God for themselves lest they discover in it the true meaning of Christian freedom and the hypocrisy of proslavery arguments based on the Bible.[29] Concerted efforts were made to prevent slaves from learning to read, but the efforts were only partly successful, and slaves discovered in Scripture a manual of liberation. In their own ecclesial gatherings, often held at night and in secret locations, there occurred what might be described as a "clearing of freedom" within the harsh domain of oppression—a clearing in which slaves were transformed into human beings, seemingly silent and docile masses into a singing, resistant, hopeful people. Theologically one can only say that the slaves experienced in a powerful way the liberating presence of the risen Christ, and indeed they gave expression to that in song and sermon.

The same continued to be true after the end of slavery. Under the conditions of segregation and marginalization, blacks found their true dignity and identity precisely and only in the black church—in that space of freedom cleared on Sunday morning and Wednesday evening, or whenever the community gathered. To "have church," as it was expressed, was to experience the presence of the Holy Spirit in the midst of the people, "empowering them with courage and strength to bear witness in their present existence to what they know is coming in God's own eschatological future."[30] The black church was, and still is, a spiritual, eschatological, transformative event that has proved to be constitutive of the very survival of a people. As such it is a paradigm of what the church might be or become for all people, and it offers rich resources for ecclesial reflection.

After the Civil War the invisible institution became for the most part a "nation within a nation."[31] It did not escape certain ambiguities in this role. During the post-Reconstruction era, when white supremacy was reestablished, the black church was to a degree co-opted by the white power structure and became an instrument of social control. The church offered a refuge in the hostile white world, serving a cathartic and compensatory function. The white man did not invade this sanctuary so long as it did not threaten his position but instead aided blacks to accommodate to their inferior status. Increasingly the churches played a practical managerial role in the life of the black community by offering essential civic services (education, health care, job training, political organization), and the struggle for liberation was postponed. Cultural isolation and social deprivation spawned cultic deviation, such as the movements of Marcus Garvey and Father Divine. Some churches were dominated by an authoritarian, anti-intellectual, self-serving male leadership. Women played an essential role in the churches but never in leadership positions. The civil-rights and black-power movements of the sixties and seventies challenged the complacency of the black churches even as these movements in large measure originated in and were nurtured by the churches.

An ambiguity of another sort is associated with the struggle for integration, in that the black churches could be threatened by integration with the loss of their distinctive identity, or at least of their isolated roles. The social world of urban and suburban blacks is becoming more complex as the black community gradually and often painfully enters the American mainstream—in a process for the moment slowed if not reversed by the not so benign neglect, indeed brutal indifference, of current social policy. One fervently hopes that as the black churches enter the ecclesial mainstream they will bring with them their distinctive qualities, helping to transform the whole, enabling their paradigm of what it means to be a church to become productive for all people. A *truly integrated* Christian church in North America would be something radically different from anything we now know. The fact is that the mainstream Protestant churches, despite changes in their official policies, remain one of the strongest bastions of racial separation and prejudice, to say nothing of class and sexual division. Blacks who are members of the majority denominations are for the moment surviving and exerting their influence through caucuses. Changes are occurring in church leadership, to be sure, and the reunion of major denominations can only have a beneficial effect, but the actual effects in local parishes, and the emergence of interracial congregations, are painfully slow in coming.

Latin American Base Communities

Latin American liberation theology has had a profound impact on all major theological topics, including questions of method (the relation of theory and praxis), anthropology, Christology, and the theology of history, but its most creative contribution has come at the point of ecclesiology. It is in many respects an ecclesiocentric theology. During the past fifteen years, and especially since about 1980, a number of important works on our topic have been published in English translation—undoubtedly the richest contribution to ecclesiology of any theological movement of our time.[32]

The three major Latin American theologians are Gustavo Gutiérrez, of Peru; Juan Luis Segundo, of Uruguay; and Leonardo Boff, of Brazil. All three are Catholic priests, all completed their theological studies in Europe, where they were shaped by the leading post–Vatican II theologians (notably Karl Rahner, Edward Schillebeeckx, and J. B. Metz), all are scholars of international reputation and quality, and all are also folk theologians who have lived and worked closely with the oppressed poor of their countries, giving voice to the grass-roots theology of the people. Liberation theology has been primarily a Catholic accomplishment in Latin America, but there are also some important Protestant voices, notably José Míguez-Bonino, of Argentina, and Rubem Alves, of Brazil. All of these thinkers, Protestant as well as Catholic, are incredibly courageous. They have attacked the political and ecclesiastical authorities directly and boldly. They are not intimidated by the Vatican nor by military dictatorships nor by United States foreign policy. They do not modulate their criticism because of strategic considerations, as many in North America do; their situation does not permit it. Their lives and positions are in constant danger. Is it any wonder that they are attracted to Dietrich Bonhoeffer as a model for theological existence today?[33]

The Second Vatican Council, with its "Dogmatic Constitution on the Church" (*Lumen Gentium*), opened up the theological possibility of a new ecclesiology. Along with the "Pastoral Constitution on the Modern World" (*Gaudium et Spes*), it was the most progressive of the conciliar documents, in which many of the leading European theologians had a hand. The Vatican reforms were concretized for the Latin American situation and extended in their implications by the first council of Latin American bishops, at Medellín in 1968. The practical possibility of—and demand for—a new ecclesiology was provided by the base ecclesial communities, the *comunidades eclesiais de base.* The word *base,* in Portuguese and Spanish as well as English, derives from the Latin *basis* and has several semantic overtones: the lowest part or bottom of a thing ("base"); that which is fundamental or essential ("basic"); that from which a start is made ("base of operations"); and, in a wordplay from Vulgar Latin, something of low esteem, ignoble, humble. The base ecclesial communities are all of these things and more. They emerged in Brazil in the late fifties and early sixties as lay evangelization movements among the poor that arose as a result of a shortage of priests and an alienation from the hierarchical upper-class church, which was part of the oppressive power structure. From the beginning they were oriented to problems of education, illiteracy, health and child care, unemployment, and job training as well as to problems of religious life. They were total communities, which gathered in any available space, sometimes without shelter of any kind. Through a system of networking, they spread rapidly through the metropolitan slums of Brazil, and by 1981 the number of communities had reached some eighty thousand. Although this was a revolution from below, a genuine grass-roots movement, its leaders often came from the privileged and educated classes. Often they were lawyers, teachers, physicians, priests, and nuns who relinquished their class privileges and lived among the people in the urban slums and rural villages. The leaders did not bring information and concepts to the people; rather these emerged from the groups themselves through a process of consciousness-raising or "conscientization" *(conscientização).*[34] The base communities became a political force with the power to mobilize an entire slum or agrarian district. In Brazil they have remained nonviolent and pacifist, but in Nicaragua and elsewhere in Central America the communities have sometimes become bases for guerrilla training.[35]

The term "ecclesiogenesis," *eclesiogênese,* did not originate with Boff but came into use at the first of several interchurch meetings of the base ecclesial communities of Brazil in 1975. It is a marvelously expressive term, comparable to *conscientização* and *comunidades eclesiais de base*—all gifts of the Portuguese language to international theological reflection. Three elements of Latin American ecclesiogenesis are contributing to a theology of the church in the new paradigm.

The church viewed as sacramental and communal rather than as juridical and hierarchical. In *A Theology of Liberation,* Gutiérrez calls for an "uncentering" of the church, which must cease thinking of itself as the exclusive place of salvation and orient itself toward a new and radical service to people.[36] This involves a return to the mission of the early Christian communities as over against post-Constantinian ecclesiocentrism; it entails a sacramental rather than an ecclesiocentric or juridical view of the church. The church is the "sacrament of history," a visible sign or sacrament of God's universally available salvation, the fulfillment of which the church announces and anticipates. The church should *be* a place of liberation and serve the *world* in the struggle for liberation. Boff develops this idea further by suggesting that the concept of sacrament expresses the oneness of the universal church (which is the mystery of salvation) with particular and quite different historical churches.[37] This is a unity in and through the Spirit, not through ecclesiastical structures.

As the sacrament of history, the church is fundamentally a redeemed, transfigured *community.* Boff proposes that we think of community as "society's utopia." As such, community never exists in a pure state but is borne, so to speak, by social and institutional structures, whose purpose is to serve it rather than vice versa: "Christianity, with its values rooted in love, forgiveness, solidarity, the renunciation of oppressive powers, the acceptance of others, and so on, is essentially oriented to the creation, within societal structures, of the communitarian spirit."[38] This community is a *communitas fidelium:* faith constitutes the minimum constitutive reality of the church, its "catholic" identity, and faith is given essentially as communion. Where such faith is present, in community, there the church universal is present, even in the tiniest base community.[39]

Boff points out that the base ecclesial communities signify a rebirth of the church from below, from the bottom up, from the base, the grass roots, not from the top down. In this connection he provides a sharply delineated comparison of the hierarchical and communal models of being church. The church cannot of course exist without an organizational structure, but hierarchy must not be allowed to establish the model or pattern. In place of a vertically linear model, we should think of a circular, or interactive, or triangular one.[40] Hierarchy is in fact so deeply embedded in Western consciousness that it is difficult for us to think of an organizational structure of any kind in nonhierarchical terms, although clearly there are other possibilities, which other cultures may help disclose to us. One of the ironies of modern secularism is that in corporations, government bureaucracies, and academic institutions, the graded "sacred rule," or hierarchy, of the Roman church has been closely imitated.

Protestants undoubtedly recognize much that is familiar here. The Reformation began as a rebirth of the church from below, it attacked the abuses of the Roman hierarchy, it fastened on to the central image of the church as a *congregatio fidelium,* and it developed a critical, paradigmatic principle. "Reformation" is another name for ecclesiogenesis—*ecclesia reformata et semper reformanda* (the church reformed and always reforming).[41] But in time the Protestant churches came to imitate in many respects the mother church. They developed hierarchical, bureaucratic structures and dogmatic, credal authorities of their own. The Bible became their pope. Worst of all, they proved to have little resistance to sociological, cultural captivity. Perhaps this was partially the result of lacking a truly sacramental understanding of ecclesia and placing too great a stress on the pure Word—a word so pure that it could be abstracted from praxis and reduced to doctrinal purity and personal morality. The second reformation of the church from below, from the Third World, from the underside of history, has a great deal to add to the first. It is much more radically "from below" than the first, which really occurred more "from within" Western culture than from below and outside it.

Eucharist and human solidarity: Political implications of ecclesiology. Not only is the church sacramental but also, according to the Latin American theologians, the sacramental is conjoined with the political. The church "takes place" where the celebration of the Lord's Supper and the creation of human solidarity are indissolubly joined. Gutiérrez points out[42] that the background of the Eucharist is political: the Jewish Passover (which celebrates the exodus from Egypt and the Sinai covenant) and the crucifixion of Jesus. Sin, he says, is the destruction of communion with God and among human beings through injustice and exploitation. Out of this central eucharistic experience there must emerge both a prophetic *denunciation* of every dehumanizing situation and an *annunciation* of the gospel in word and deed—not abstractly but within a commitment to liberation, in concrete solidarity with people and the exploited classes. Gutiérrez acknowledges that such a denunciation and annunciation may run the risk of politicizing the gospel, but he thinks the risk cannot be avoided by attempting to hide the real political implications of the gospel (that is a different kind of politicization). Rather, it is necessary to go to the very roots of the problem: "It is where the annunication of the Gospel seems to border on submersion into the purely historical realm that there must be born the reflection, the spirituality, and the new preaching of a Christian message which is incarnated—not lost—in our here and now."[43]

The dominant political and economic reality in Latin America today is the result, in the view of liberation theology, of an international capitalism that has exported its most abusive features to the Third World, exploiting cheap labor and maintaining a plutocratic power structure (aristocratic, managerial-technocratic, military). It has created a situation of class struggle and conflict for which Marxist analysis is especially helpful. This is partly the result of the fact that a large and stable industrially based middle class was never able to develop in Latin America as it did in Europe and North America. Without a middle class—the much-maligned bourgeoisie—there could only be a continuous and radical polarization between the elite and the oppressed. To pass into a postbourgeois, postindustrial culture without having first passed through the bourgeois, industrial age involves radical and unprecedented social revolution. Consequently Marxism has had a following among Latin American intellectuals that far exceeds its influence in North America or Western Europe.[44] The major theologians—Segundo, Gutiérrez, Boff, Míquez-Bonino, and others—are in conversation with Marxists, but it would be naive and irresponsible to suggest that they themselves are Marxists. They know that one cannot simply *be* both Christian and Marxist, since Marxism as an ideology rejects the validity of all religion, regarding it as a palliative for social oppression. They are critical of Marxism's analytic oversimplifications, and they have no interest in importing Soviet and Eastern-bloc state socialism into Latin America. That would be to substitute one abusive system for another. The "socialist option" they envision is something quite distinct from anything the world has known. To reject this as utopian is simply to caricature the nuanced and politically sophisticated discussion of these issues,[45] as well as to exhibit an appalling lack of imagination. In brief, one could say that for these theologians, Marxism is part of the work of denunciation, not of annunciation.

The preferential option for the poor. The phrase "preferential option for the poor" comes from one of the documents of the second conference of Latin American bishops, held in Puebla in 1979.[46] Like liberation theology, this conference was preoccupied with the problem of poverty, which as Gutiérrez has pointed out, is a complex phenomenon with several aspects. In *A Theology of Liberation,*[47] he distinguishes between material poverty, spiritual poverty, and poverty as a commitment of solidarity and protest. *Material poverty* is, from the biblical point of view, a scandalous, degrading condition, inimical to human dignity, contrary to the will of God. The prophetic critique of poverty in ancient Israel has been demonstrated through studies by Roland de Vaux, Norman K. Gottwald, José Miranda, and others. The poor are blessed, according to the gospel, not because of their poverty but because God's kingdom is near, the kingdom that means the end of exploitation and poverty and other forms of dehumanization. *Poverty as spiritual childhood* entails a radical openness to God, a condition of not being attached to material goods even if one possesses them. It is an aspect of the "spirituality of liberation" to which Gutiérrez has directed his attention more fully in recent writings.[48] The material and spiritual meanings of poverty are joined in *poverty as a commitment of solidarity and protest.* If material poverty is something to be rejected, then a witness of poverty cannot make it a Christian ideal. Spiritual poverty as total availability to the Lord must be oriented to the problem of material poverty. Just as Jesus' solidarity with sin was not to idealize it but to redeem from it, so our spiritual solidarity with material poverty is not to idealize it but to liberate from it. One cannot really be with the poor unless one is struggling and protesting against poverty. Hence this solidarity must manifest itself in specific actions and life styles that can, of course, take a number of different forms. The most demanding and surely the most valuable is that of actually living and working with the poor, as several of the Latin American theologians have chosen to do. But only a few are capable of this severe discipline; for others, indeed most, it may be possible, helpful, and legitimate to engage in political action or social and educational leadership aimed at raising consciousness and bringing about structural change, so long as one recognizes this to be a lesser way, involving necessary compromises.

But why a *preferential option* for the poor? Should not the ecclesial community be open to and minister to the needs of all, regardless of social class? Of course. The affluent suffer in different ways—satiety, anomie, waste, boredom, loss of meaning, drugs and alcohol, divorce and suicide, to mention a few. But the suffering of the affluent is for the most part self-inflicted rather than imposed by others. Their need is not as great, and there is a simple, obvious sense in which one helps the most those who need help the most—although there is also a strange sense in which those who have the least are able to give the most. Hegel pointed out that the initiative in breaking the master-slave relationship lies with the slaves, not the masters.[49] Likewise, the initiative in breaking the dichotomy between the rich and the poor and overcoming poverty must lie with the poor, not the rich. The rich, the masters, and the oppressors are more enslaved to the system they have created than the poor, and they cannot free themselves through their own initiative. They are dependent on the labor and poverty of the oppressed in ways that the oppressed are not dependent on them. Individuals can, of course, break free, but the structure itself will not change of its own accord. It will change only when it is effectively challenged from without or from below.

So if one wants to transform the whole destructive, dehumanizing structure, one opts for the poor. But that option for the poor is in fact an option for the whole of humanity. "This means," writes Rosemary Radford Ruether,

> in the language of liberation theology, that God as liberator acts in history to liberate all through opting for the poor and the oppressed of the present system. The poor, the downcast, those who hunger and thirst, have a certain priority in God's work of redemption. Part of the signs of the kingdom is that the lame walk, the blind see, the captives are freed, the poor have the gospel preached to them. Christ goes particularly to the outcasts, and they, in turn, have a special affinity for the gospel. But the aim of this partiality is to create a new whole, to elevate the valleys and make the high places low, so that all may come into a new place of God's reign, when God's will is done on earth.[50]

Troeltsch argued that all great religious movements based on divine revelation and containing prophetic, redemptive power have originated among the poor, the lower classes. "They alone unite imagination and simplicity of feeling with a non-reflective habit of mind, a primitive energy, and an urgent sense of need." So it was with Christianity. "Jesus himself was a man of the people, and his gospel bears clear traces of the simple peasant and artisan conditions of Galilee. It is only the poor and humble who easily understand his gospel; it is difficult for the rich and for the religious leaders because they do not feel their need." Troeltsch went on to point out that in the case of a new faith containing deep religious power, "the early naive religious content always fuses with all the highest religious forces of the intellectual culture of the day; apart from this fusion faith would be broken by the impact of the cultural environment."[51] So too it was with Christianity, which soon developed a sophisticated theology and transcended all social distinctions. But at the beginning, and also at times of renewal, it is the poor who "have a special affinity for the gospel." The great Christian reform movements have also often come from the lower classes. Thus the base ecclesial communities are playing a special role in the ecclesial rebirth of our time.

The Feminist Ecclesial Vision[52]

Feminist theology and the feminist liberation movement are having a profound impact on the life and thought of the church. It is true that until recently, the struggle against patriarchalism and sexism has not achieved a distinctive institutionalization in the same sense that the black struggle against racism has institutionalized itself in the black churches and that the Latin American struggle against economic injustice and class oppression has institutionalized itself in the base ecclesial communities. For the most part, the institutionalization of the feminist church struggle is occurring within the established churches as they gradually undergo change. But now a new form of institutionalization of the struggle is emerging that will prove to be of far-reaching significance, namely, the "women-church" movement or "feminist exodus communities" that are forming both within and at the edges of existing church institutions.

A large body of feminist theological literature already exists, and it is growing rapidly. But until recently, relatively little attention has been directed to ecclesial questions in the strict sense. In my judgment, the two scholars who have made the most substantial contribution to a feminist theology of the church are Elisabeth Schüssler Fiorenza and Rosemary Radford Ruether.[53] In certain respects their work is complementary; both of their perspectives are needed, and I shall draw upon them in turn for the first and the second of the three issues to be immediately considered. It should be clear this discussion is limited to Christian feminism. Post-Christian feminism represents an external challenge and alternative not only to the church but to Christian faith as such, even if in the separatist communities of women who have turned away from Christianity, or who never affirmed it, some striking traces of Christian sectarianism as an alienated heritage may be detected.[54]

Three elements are influential in forming a feminist ecclesial vision today, and they also contribute significantly to a theology of the church in the new paradigm: (*a*) a discovery of the egalitarian and inclusive character of many of the early Christian communities; (*b*) the changing role of women in church leadership, including the emergence of the women-church movement; and (*c*) the revolution in language.

Discovery of early egalitarianism. One of the crucial factors in supporting the advocacy of a Christian feminist theology has been the discovery that the Christian movement was at its point of origin radically egalitarian and inclusive, representing a subversive reversal of prevailing social patterns in Jewish and Hellenistic culture, and that women played a role in the founding of Christianity and in early church leadership. While repatriarchalization occurred very quickly, and along with it the emergence of misogynist attitudes, the "clearing of freedom" that occurred at the very beginning provides a basis for advancing theological claims concerning the essence of the ecclesial community—a transfigured, liberated, inclusive community. If it were otherwise—if it were to be found that Christianity *as such,* at its *core,* were sexist, racist, classist —then those committed to human liberation could no longer be Christian. The Christian religion would not be retrievable; it would have to be rejected as false. This is in effect the view of radical, post-Christian feminism. The debate here is primarily over historical matters and their proper interpretation. Just as post-Enlightenment Protestant liberal theology had the courage to subject its faith to the probing questions raised by historical criticism, so too has contemporary feminist theology. Of course the truth of faith cannot be *demonstrated* by historical evidence, but it can be *falsified.* The claims of a historical religion can be severely damaged if its historical foundations are eroded or destroyed by critical investigations. Part of the risk of faith is the willingness to engage in this kind of honest probing without predetermined results.

The hermeneutical problem is that virtually all biblical texts are products of an androcentric, patriarchal culture and share in the distortions of that culture, even if unintentionally. Thus it cannot be the texts as such that constitute the revelatory heart of Christianity for feminists but (if anything at all) something that "lurks" behind or beneath them.[55] Yet these texts are the only texts we have, and if they are denied or rejected outright, we are left empty-handed. Thus Schüssler Fiorenza argues that precisely these texts must be "reclaimed" as women's own revelatory texts and history; they must be made to allow a glimpse of the early Christian movement as a "discipleship of equals" and of the "basileia vision of Jesus as the praxis of inclusive wholeness."[56] The method she employs includes the familiar tools of form and redaction criticism, but they are employed from a different interpretive perspective, a feminist critical perspective, which allows the seeing of hitherto hidden or unnoticed things from a different angle of vision.

Schüssler Fiorenza's "reconstruction of Christian origins" focuses on three major elements: the Jesus movement, the early Christian missionary movement, and Pauline theology.[57] With respect to the first, her conclusions are similar to those of a number of other feminists, and they are based upon a rigorous exegesis of the texts by an accomplished biblical scholar. Central to the Jesus movement, she argues, is the "basileia vision" enunciated in Jesus' parables and sayings—the vision of a new way of being communally human in the world through God's redemptive presence —together with Jesus' praxis of healing and fellowship oriented especially to three groups of people: the destitute poor; the sick and crippled; tax collectors, sinners, and prostitutes. Women were included in this fellowship and played a central role in recognizing and identifying who Jesus was—the unnamed woman at Bethany who anointed him, Mary Magdalene, the other women disciples who were faithful to Jesus at the cross and were the first witnesses of the resurrection. The important point here is not the historicist argument that unless it can be shown that women were included as equals by Jesus and the earliest community, they do not have a claim to equality in the church now. Rather, the fact of the inclusion of women, as the largest and most visible of the marginalized groups in the Palestinian world, is indicative of something essential about the ministry of Jesus and the ecclesial community that emerged from it: its essentially nonprovincial, open character, its inclusion of all people without any conditions whatsoever in the basileia vision, its prophetic denouncement of all divisions based on status, privilege, religious piety, sex, ethnic group, and so on. On the basis of the inclusion of women, the inclusion of marginalized groups who were not present or visible in the time of Jesus, such as racial minorities or homosexuals, must also be affirmed.

With respect to the early Christian missionary movement, the hermeneutical problem is one of getting behind the Pauline and deutero-Pauline texts and the text of Acts, to the pre-Pauline Hellenistic Jewish-Christian communities and the missionary movement associated with them. Schüssler-Fiorenza's critical reconstruction of that milieu is a scholarly contribution of great importance. She focuses on the missionaries, the house church, and the theological self-understanding of these early communities.[58] First, it is clear that the early Christian missionary movement allowed for the full participation and leadership of women, working either singly or in partnership with men. A number of names are mentioned—Phoebe, Prisca, Junia, Apphia, Euodia, Syntyche, Mary, Tryphaena, Tryphosa, Persis—and it is very likely that this is only the tip of a hidden iceberg. Second, the primary institutionalization of these communities was in the form of the house church, and since women were among the wealthy and prominent converts to Christianity, they played an important role in the founding, sustaining, and leading of such house churches, where Christians could gather without regard to sex or social status for the purpose of *diakonia* (the communal meal) and *liturgeia* (the service and praise of God).

Finally, the theological self-understanding of the communities was rooted in the experience of the Spirit. The communities tended, moreover, to understand the ministry and life of Jesus in terms of his being the Wisdom of God. The words for "spirit" in Hebrew and "wisdom" in Greek are grammatically feminine and can serve as feminine images of the divine. The communities adopted a prophetic-critical attitude toward the temple as the locus of divine presence, and understood the household of God to be the new eschatological temple in which all are included and all are equal—Jews, Gentiles, women, men, slaves, the free poor, the rich, those with high status and those who are nothing in the eyes of the world. Schüssler Fiorenza concludes that the famous proclamation of Gal. 3:28—". . . neither Jew nor Greek, neither slave nor free, neither male nor female, all are one in Christ Jesus"—belongs to *this* theological setting. It is a key expression not of Pauline theology as such (Paul borrowed and refined it) but of the theological self-understanding of the early Christian missionary movement. The fact that it was present at the beginning has a fundamental significance for claims regarding what is truly distinctive about the Christian ecclesia.

On the one hand, Paul adopted this radical vision, giving it theological depth and substance. But on the other hand, he introduced certain qualifications and modifications. He preferred that Christian missionaries remain unmarried, and he restricted the participation of married women as missionaries and in community worship. His use of the virgin-bride metaphor for the church, as well as his figurative characterization of his apostleship as fatherhood, opened the door for a reintroduction of patriarchal values and sexual dualities. He was more concerned, finally, about maintaining order and preventing misinterpretation of the Christian assemblies as orgiastic cults than he was about the equality and participation of all women, married as well as unmarried. And he did not draw the full social and political implications of his radical theological vision; because of his so-called eschatological proviso, his belief that this world would shortly end. To be sure, the conditions for radical social change were not present in the ancient world. But had Paul realized that these reservations would open the door for the reintroduction of patriarchy, hierarchy, sexism, and racism into the church, he would very likely have been astonished.[59]

Women in church leadership. There may have indeed been a "clearing of freedom" at the beginning of the Christian movement, but was not this quickly subverted by an all too familiar pattern of the "promise and betrayal"[60] of women throughout Christian history? Origins, crucial as they are, are not enough. If the subsequent history of the church is an utter betrayal of its founding moment, and if there are no possibilities for the transformation and revisioning of this history, then there is no reason why women in quest of liberation should identify themselves as Christians. The story is indeed bleak, but not utterly so. Although the emergent hierarchical structure of the church was male and increasingly celibate and misogynist, and although women were often brutally marginalized, there was a subversive undercurrent that was never completely suppressed and that is being recovered today by detailed historical studies.[61] Against all odds, women did repeatedly assume positions of leadership in the church, often, to be sure, on the fringe, but a fringe that served as an important corrective to the patriarchal mainstream—in Gnosticism and Montanism, medieval spirituality, post-Reformation sectarian movements (e.g., the Shakers and Quakers), and Christian utopian and socialist communities. These fringe groups—often denounced as heretical—and the women involved in them helped keep alive an undistorted vision of what the church might be.

Today the situation is changing dramatically and women are increasingly assuming leadership positions in the mainstream churches and in religious studies. American Protestant women have in the past fifteen years rapidly increased their numbers in theological seminaries, and at several of the liberal and ecumenical schools they are now in the majority. Roman Catholic women are also entering theological education in surprising numbers considering the lack of career options for them in their church at the present time. Clearly a ferment is at work among both Catholic and Protestant women that could have a profound impact on the future of the church.

The ordination of women by Protestant churches and the growing presence of women in the ordained ministry of several Protestant denominations mark a major accomplishment and show the possibility of even more radical changes. But there is no guarantee of these changes. The churches might simply turn to women out of necessity or desperation as men abandon the ministry because of poor salaries, low status, or continuing job frustration; then very little would change. Or the profession might become "feminized" in a stereotypical fashion, attracting traditional women who are willing to continue functioning in traditional role models. Everything depends on the *kind* of women, and men, who assume positions of church leadership in the future. Will they be willing and able to challenge and transform a still quite massively patriarchal institution that is unlikely to change until it is forced to change? Patriarchy is a social system in which the "fathers"—that is, ruling-class males—hold the positions of power, and historical experience teaches us that those who hold power are rarely willing to relinquish it voluntarily. In brief, both church and ministry must be fundamentally revisioned if women are to participate in them on the basis of equality. This revisioning must occur not only in the Catholic church, where it is clear that the hierarchy is organizing for a protracted struggle against the ordination of women, but also in the Protestant churches, where tokenism dulls the cutting edge of change and encourages accommodationism.

It is here that the women-church movement is of critical importance.[62] As Ruether points out, "autonomous bases" are needed —feminist base ecclesial communities, in effect[63]—in order to enable women to "collectivize their own experience and form a critical counterculture to patriarchy." Without the consciousness-raising, the nurturing, the liturgical celebration, and the mutual support provided by such communities, it will be very difficult for women to sustain themselves in the struggle, especially since they will often find themselves isolated and in the minority among church leadership in the mainstream institutions. Ruether makes it clear that the need for separate bases (on the part not only of women but also of blacks and other minorities and the poor) should not be confused with "ideological separatism," which in the case of women is generally accompanied by a dualistic anthropology that denies to males the capacity for authentic humanity. Separation is not an end in itself but a necessary stage in a dialectical process of transformation—a process whose end is no longer women-church but simply church, the "authentic community of exodus from oppression" in all its forms and for all people.[64] Moreover, the separation practiced by women-church is by no means total. Individual women will pass back and forth between the feminist base communities and the rest of their lives (including traditional church activities) in a variety of ways, and much of their time will continue to be spent in the presence of men.

Men have sometimes raised the question whether they may participate in women-church if they desire. The question is in certain respects unnecessary, since any authentic manifestation of ecclesia is inclusive. But men should respect the appropriateness of the moment of separation in the dialectic of reconciliation, recognizing the need for women to establish autonomous bases and the danger of subversion by a male presence, even if well intentioned. Men who find themselves unable to participate in the traditional church because of its patriarchal attitudes should of course be welcome in the women-church.

The feminist communities are determined to understand themselves as "exodus communities" *within* and *on the edges* of the institution, refusing to leave it as sectarian or schismatic groups but also refusing to fit into it on its own terms, working to transform it without being stifled or controlled by it. In this respect women-church follows a traditional Catholic pattern of remaining within the *ecclesia catholica* rather than the Protestant sectarian pattern of starting a new church. Women-church is an "institution" only in a loose sense; it has more the character of a grass-roots movement in which local groups form spontaneously and for which there is only a skeletal organization but an active communications network.

Women-church, as long as it remains true to its own vision, can be viewed as a paradigm of what the church as a whole should become, a sign and sacrament of ecclesial wholeness beyond all patriarchy, all clericalism, all misogynism. The same is true of the black church as a paradigm of the church beyond all racial prejudice, and of the Latin American base communities as a paradigm beyond all class oppression. We have noted that a truly racially integrated Christian church in America would be some-thing quite radically different from anything we now know. The same would be true of a church in which all divisions between classes had been decisively repudiated and in which all traces of patriarchy and sexism had been truly overcome. It is a radical vision, but nothing less is expected of us. These are paradigms of the church of the future.

The revolution in language. During the past decade, seminaries and churches have been experiencing a veritable revolution in the use of language. It is more evident in the seminaries than in the churches, more evident in religious studies than in other academic disci-plines, more evident in the academy than in the general culture. But here, as with the feminist movement as a whole, we are at only the beginning of sweeping changes that normally have required decades or even centuries to become well established.

Language is close to the heart of things: it is not merely a way of speaking but a way of being and thinking and acting: people *live* by images and symbols. That is why language is so difficult to change and why the opposition to change is often so emotionally charged. But most people who have participated in the language revolution have discovered that far from being some faddish distortion of tradition, it is bringing us closer to central meanings of the Christian gospel and ecclesial existence.

Symptomatic of the resistance to change is adherence to masculine imagery for God, notably the word "father." But this very symbol is not static. In primitive consciousness, God was closely associated with the dominant, authoritative father figure, a father who was to be both revered and feared, a protector and a rival. The relationship was described by Freud as Oedipal. But the symbol grew and was transformed by Hebraic and Christian tradition. The Abba of Jesus' proclamation transcended the psychic, familial, and sexual context from which the symbol emerged; this father was a friend, a companion, a fellow sufferer, in some respects a motherlike father. The context was no longer archaic but eschatological, for the fatherhood of this God was to be exercised through the inbreaking basileia.[65] Giving up one sort of relationship to God—essentially an infantile relationship to the father—makes possible another sort of relationship, an ecclesial relationship. The feminist linguistic revolution has helped us see and understand this more clearly. The very things of which the feminist theologians are most critical—patriarchalism, sexism, authoritarianism, clericalism—are marks of a lingering infantilism, the temptation of religion to regress to its archaic roots, a temptation that must be resisted again and again if the church is to be an inclusive, egalitarian community.

This does not mean that all the old symbols of God must be abandoned, but it does mean adopting a critical consciousness toward them, reconfiguring and supplementing them through a creative exercise of the religious imagination.[66] There is finally no inclusive language for God. Every symbol of the transcendent is relative, finite, limited, exclusive of some things just as it affirms others. Thus we must learn to think and speak of God dialectically, critically, symbolically, and in a multiplicity of ways. A wholesale abandonment of traditional language would be foolhardy, because there is much beauty, power, wisdom, truth, and eloquence in it. To speak "humbly" of our God calls for a multiplication and enrichment of language, not its impoverishment or its reduction to puritan formulas. In the ecclesia of freedom we are to "make a joyful noise to the Lord."

3. ECUMENISM, WORLD CHRISTIANITY, AND
ENCOUNTER AMONG THE RELIGIONS

The third item on the agenda of a theology of the church in the new paradigm is a complex of issues arising in part from an inexorable historical process—the growth in economic and techno-logical interdependence among the peoples of the world. This growth has undoubtedly spurred the development of an ecumenical movement among separated Christians and a heightened awareness that Christianity is a global religion of many different shapes. But at the same time it has had the negative consequence of encouraging the trend toward privatism, provincialism, and exclusiveness that is so widespread today, hindering among other things precisely an ecumenical attitude. For without a spiritual basis for unity and cooperation, material interdependence only heightens tensions and conflicts, causing people to become more defensive and fearful.[67] The very things that provide a material basis for the unification of humanity—rapid transportation, instant communication, ad-vanced technologies, multinational corporations, international trade, cultural interdependence—also threaten it. Something is missing, something that could be provided by the religions through an engagement in reciprocal dialogue and encounter.

I shall attempt to get at this complex of issues through a series of ten theses, some of which are formulated rather polemically with the hope of eliciting discussion.

1. There is a widespread complacency today about the divided state of the Christian churches. Most Protestants accept their denominations as something normative and sacrosanct. The Roman Catholic hierarchy has an ambivalent attitude toward genuine ecumenical relations with other Christian communions, despite the openings provided by the Second Vatican Council. The Orthodox churches are suspicious of and on the defensive against modernity. Evangelicals and conservatives are more interested in purity of doctrine and morals than in Christian unity, the advocacy of which they tend to regard as a subversive plot. College and seminary students are no longer involved in the ecumenical move-ment with conviction and knowledge. Rarely is it openly acknowl-edged that division among Christians is a scandal, a shameful, sinful situation, something contrary to the will of God.

2. The Protestant Reformation had negative as well as positive consequences.[68] Most Protestants think of the Reformation as an unambiguous good, a necessary and wholly justified correction of Roman Catholic abuses, and they tend to view Protestantism as the only true form of the church. But there were negative consequences as well, the effects of which are still with us. These include the religious wars of the sixteenth and seventeenth centuries which

divided Europe, denominational and sectarian rivalries, wasted resources and duplication of effort, and the growth of modern secularism. There are of course many causes of secularism, but one of them has been the divisions among the Christian churches. When Christianity could no longer provide a basis for communal unity and identity, new bases were found in regional, national, cultural, and ethnic ideologies. In its divided state, Christianity has tended to lose credibility and to waste its resources, both economic and intellectual. There are too many seminaries, too much infighting, too little fundamental thinking and transformative praxis.

The real issues today cut across denominational and confessional lines, and the creative theology of our time is ecumenical theology. Though the great theological traditions (e.g., Catholic, Lutheran, Reformed, Orthodox, Anglican, Baptist, Free church) continue to provide important resources for theological reflection, it is an anachronism to attempt to perpetuate them in their specific confessional forms. Since the intention of the Reformers was to reform the Catholic church, not divide it, it can be argued that the work of the Reformation will not be finished until Christians are reunited in a church that is at once truly reformed and truly catholic.

3. The exigency for unity does not reside in scriptural proofs or even in appeals to the classic "mark" of unity but in the fundamental logic of Christian faith, which is oriented to a single central figure and event (God's redemptive action in Christ) and which is intrinsically nonprovincial in character (legitimizing no divisions or exclusions on the basis of race, sex, creed, nationality, locale, or language). Establishing this is a matter not of appeals to authority but of argument from the essence of Christianity. The burden of proof rests upon those who contend that a given state of circumstances justifies or makes unavoidable division, schism, or separation. I do not deny that such circumstances may sometimes exist, but they represent a failure of the church, a grievous loss.

4. The basis for Christian unity is simply the confession of faith in Jesus as the Christ, not unity of creed, doctrine, or polity. Creeds and theologies are attempts at understanding what the confession of faith in Christ means under different historical circumstances and in relation to specific issues. As such they are relative and partial. Unity cannot be based on a common creed, or on doctrinal

purity, or on biblical literalism, or on magisterial authority. To be
sure, all or most Christians may be able to assent to the Apostles'
Creed, but only as a traditional affirmation in a liturgical context,
not as a contemporary specification of faith in light of current
controversies. Today the Apostles' Creed must be *interpreted*, and
the interpretations will vary. The same is true of all the church's
creeds, as well as its Scriptures.

5. The precondition of Christian unity is the recognition and
acceptance of diversity, plurality, and difference. The ecumenical
goal is *unity in diversity*, not uniformity. Unity does not reduce
diversity but rather demands and allows it. In as complex a human
activity as religion, there can be no unity on any other terms. The
human possibilities of expression, experimentation, and imagina-
tive variation are just too rich to demand anything like monolithic
conformity. Those who cannot tolerate diversity of creed, interpretation, practice, structure, and the like, must insist on separation in order to preserve a rigid identity, and between the
separated branches there reign mutual suspicion and hostility.
True unity enriches diversity and creativity rather than sup-
pressing it. True identity is achieved not through adherence
to rigid formulas but through the conflict and interplay of interpretations.

In this respect unity is very much like love, for love demands the
recognition of difference and its preservation even as it is taken up
into unity. Love means entering into a self-transforming relationship with that which is genuinely, and perhaps radically, other. Like
love, unity is a dialectical act. It is not easy or natural. It is one of
the most difficult of human activities, requiring perseverance,
discipline, openness, and faith. It is not simply a human activity
but a divine gift. Augustine located the unity of the church in love,
the love that is poured out by the Holy Spirit.

6. The ultimate goal of Christian unity is some kind of structural
union.[69]

(*a*) On the way to union, a variety of organizational options
are available: national united churches (as in Canada and India),
reunited denominations (such as the Presbyterian Church U.S.A.),
Christian world communions (e.g., the Lutheran World Federation,
the World Methodist Council), bilateral dialogues (e.g., Roman
Catholic and Baptist), partnership dialogues (e.g., United Church
of Christ and Christian Church Disciples of Christ), and councils
(e.g., the National Council of Churches, the World Council of

Churches). Here again there is no uniformity. It is clear only that the structure of any united or uniting church must be democratic, participatory, and federal. What is required is solidarity and reciprocity among equals, with no unilateral, hierarchical exercise of authority. A monolithic church today would be a historical anachronism; rather than serving the goal of the unity of humanity, it would impede it.

(b) The process of reunion must occur both from above and from below. Wolfhart Pannenberg suggests a new ecumenical council including all Christian groups on an equal basis. Liberation theologians point to the base ecclesial communities and feminists to the women-church. The Consultation on Church Union calls for both—for covenanting at all levels, from national churches to local groups.[70] Given the present climate of opinion, grass-roots movements from below are more likely to be productive.

(c) Separate confessional and ecclesial traditions must eventually die and disappear in their old forms in order to allow the full unity of the church to be born anew. Nothing less costly is demanded than a kind of death to receive a fuller life. Is it a price that denominations and traditions are willing to pay? It is a high price, but if the ecumenical goal is unity in diversity, not uniformity, then what must die out is the separateness and provincialism of the old traditions, not their special qualities and distinctive contributions to ecclesial wholeness.

(d) A genuine union is a matter not of one separated group's being merged into another (e.g., Protestants becoming Roman Catholic, Congregationalists becoming Disciples) but of a wholly new church's being born—an ecclesiogenesis—by giving up what is merely parochial from the old churches but preserving all that is worth saving. This is a radical demand, and it explains why ecumenical discussions are so difficult and protracted, requiring complex and delicate negotiations. The most difficult matters inevitably focus not on creed and communion but on polity and church offices, for these are what determine relations of power and control. Are Presbyterians willing to accept bishops, Episcopalians presbyteries, and Protestants the Petrine office? If some of these old offices are retained in a new church, they will undergo significant unforeseeable modifications.

7. Not only the ecumenical but the global character of Christianity must be recognized: it is a world religion, transcending denominations, confessions, regions, nations, and continents. Clearly

Christianity is growing most rapidly in the Third World and among nonwhite indigenous groups.[71] South America is the most populous Christian continent, and Africa by the end of the century will have a majority Christian population. The geographical center of Christianity is shifting once again, this time to the Southern Hemisphere. The balance among Christian groups is also shifting, since the growth in Latin America, Africa, and Asia is largely among Roman Catholics. During the course of the twentieth century, Protestants (including Anglicans) will have declined as a percentage of the world population from 9.4 percent in 1900 to an estimated 7.0 percent in 2000, and as a percentage of total Christians from 27.4 percent to 21.8 percent. During this same period, Roman Catholics will have risen from 16.8 to 18.7 percent of the world population, and from 48.7 to 57.9 percent of all Christians. One might think that statistics like these would promote an interest among Protestants in ecumenical dialogue and stir a recognition that the Christian church is a world church of many communions and groups. But insofar as the situation is acknowledged at all, it is more likely to evoke a defensive reaction or redoubled efforts to evangelize in the name of this or that denomination.

8. Not only is the world becoming less Protestant, it is also becoming less Western, less Christian, less religious. The challenge of secularism in the postmodern period suggests that the survival of Christianity, and perhaps the survival of humanity as such, may depend upon among other things a serious encounter among the religions of the world. During the twentieth century it is estimated that Christians will have declined as a percentage of the world population from 34.4 percent to 32.3 percent; the loss would have been much greater had it not been for rapid growth in Third World regions. Among the other great world religions, Islam has increased dramatically and Hinduism modestly, while Buddhism and Judaism have declined. The severest loss of adherents has been among folk religions and tribal religions; by far the most significant growth in the twentieth century has been in the numbers of the nonreligious and atheists, from 0.2 percent in 1900 to 21.3 percent in 2000.

The world reality reflected by these figures may only with difficulty sink into the consciousness of a nation at present experiencing an evangelical Christian revival.[72] But in light of the numbers it is not entirely inappropriate to ask whether religion as such is destined gradually to become a "thing of the past" for human consciousness, as life becomes increasingly technological, instrumental, and secular in its orientation, ideology, skills, and values. Perhaps this is the great question on the horizon of all religions. What seems to be called for is the creation of a global religious consciousness and a partnership in the struggle against common threats—technological dehumanization, militarism, nuclear war, environmental destruction, uncontrolled population growth, poverty and starvation, political and economic oppression. Nothing is more foolish in our time than religious wars or religious rivalries such as those occurring today in the Middle East and Northern Ireland. Without religion, the spiritual basis for unity among humankind will be lacking and we are likely to destroy ourselves through the conflicts engendered by the facts of interdependence. If the religions are to survive and be strengthened, they will have to learn from each other and to be mutually transformed and enriched through creative encounters.

9. The precondition of genuine encounter is the acceptance of religious pluralism.[73] The habit of placing Christianity over against all the other world religions, and of contending that it alone is the one true and revealed religion outside of which no salvation is to be found, is slowly dying.[74] This exclusivist posture was first replaced with a theory of inclusivism which argued that truth and revelation are present in other religions but also included within the Christian truth and revelation. In place of a simple opposition between Christianity, Judaism, and paganism, a developmental theory of religions was offered, with Christianity as the culmination.[75] But it is evident that inclusivism is a halfway house, since what is included is necessarily subordinated to what includes it. Most Christians, for example, would not be satisfied with the "inclusion" of Christianity by Buddhism. Pluralism, therefore, is the only consistent and intellectually defensible option—the recognition, namely, that the great world religions have equally valid claims and that each is culturally relative. There is no universal world court or absolute philosophy in which the rival truth claims can be adjudicated.[76]

10. Pluralism may be intellectually honest, but it has profound implications for the self-understanding of the Christian church, for the church's understanding of its identity and mission. This leads into the final thesis: that a deeper understanding of the nature of the ecclesial community can be gained through an encounter with other religions. We must recognize, in the first place, that an

acknowledgment of religious pluralism and cultural relativity by no means entails solipsism, relativism, or syncretism. It is in fact possible to maintain a fundamental loyalty to a relative religion, knowing that what is truth for us is not truth for all. We will find that the more deeply we trust what we believe to be true, the more open we are able to become to wisdom from any source. We may believe that there is indeed an ultimate unity of truth, but it is only partially attainable, knowable only in a plurality of forms. We can know the absolute only relatively, but this is not to deny the reality of the absolute. Rather than surrendering to a debilitating relativism, we are encouraged rather to deepen and broaden our openness to the absolute and to join others in a global struggle for liberation, justice, and truth.

John Cobb suggests that the religions can be mutually transformed through encounter and dialogue—not transformed into different religions but deepened in the realization of their own universal meanings.[77] Continuing transformation is necessary if the church is to be "always reforming." In our postmodern world, this transforming process may be increasingly sparked by contacts between world religions. One example of this, which bears directly upon the ecclesial community, comes from the dialogue between Christianity and Mahayana Buddhism. Gautama, Cobb points out, taught that we suffer because we are attached to things, and that when we relinquish this attachment we become free. The result is a freedom *for* all things because it is a complete freedom *from* all things. This detachment is more radical than anything we know in the West; it is both a total emptiness and a total fullness.

The Christian faith approximates this sense of total detachment, but it is hindered by our Western cultural heritage of possession, ownership, self-activity, and individual fulfillment. What Buddhism calls detachment, Christianity calls grace—God's salvific gift that can never be claimed or possessed but can only be accepted in thankfulness and given to others. It is an emptiness that is a fullness. Living by grace is a complete letting go, not a holding fast, an openness to what presents itself, a gaining of life only by losing it. Such grace appears to be the basic condition and constitutive reality of the ecclesial community, which is a community of reciprocity, solidarity, and mutuality of recognition, of intending the other for the sake of the other, and of mediating grace for others without preconditions or expectations. But such a community is almost a utopian ideal in our consumer-oriented, materialist, individualist culture. Perhaps Buddhism can help the Christian church to be a community of grace in a graceless culture by showing more clearly what it means to have faith without attachment, to find fulfillment in utter emptiness, to become a communal self by giving up private selfhood. The church might be helped then to become, in a fragmentary way, a gathering of those who are free, an ecclesia of freedom.

3

Toward a Theology of Ministry in the New Paradigm

What would a theology of ministry look like if the features of the new paradigm we have been discussing were taken seriously? What are the implications for ministry of our rethinking the "essence" of ecclesial community as it relates to the historicality and sociality of the church, the global struggle for liberation, the ecumenical movement within Christianity, and the encounter among world religions? This is a book about the nature of the church, not about the vocation of ministry, although it is clear that a discussion of the church apart from the question of its leadership would be incomplete, as would any treatment of ministry in isolation from a theology of the church. Yet I claim no special expertise on the topic of ministry and only limited familiarity with the immense literature on the subject.[1] Hence the reflections that follow are brief and tentative. They are set forward as a series of theses.

1. We face a crisis in church leadership today. Among Catholics there has been a drop in seminary enrollments, a severe shortage of priests in the Third World, a refusal to ordain women and permit married clergy, and a continued entrenchment of hierarchical structures and clericalist attitudes. Recent Vatican attempts to silence opposition within the priesthood, orders, and seminaries —Küng, Boff, Charles Curran, the signers of the letter in the *New York Times* on abortion—are especially ominous and can only have the effect of discouraging independently minded persons from undertaking the vocation of leadership in the Catholic church.

Among Protestants, the situation is equally serious: the profession is not attracting enough talented people, seminary education for the most part is of poor quality, ministerial salaries are

uncompetitive with the pay in most other professions, congregational expectations of leadership are often quite low and parochial,
and ministers frequently find themselves trapped in anachronistic,
personally destructive roles (such as having to exhibit an exemplary
piety that substitutes for congregational impiety). The situation
will only grow more severe as the pool of college graduates shrinks
and the best students are attracted into lucrative, if often sterile,
professions. Most discouraging is the lack of any real acknowledgment of the situation on the part of congregations, denominational
bureaucracies, and seminaries; for the most part, it is business as
usual and there is considerable resistance to any real change in the
profession on the part of those who are in it. One hopeful but
limited sign may be the growing number of second-career theological students who are turning to the ministry with a recognition of
what its potentialities are.

2. The fundamental purpose of ministry is to guide and serve the
process of ecclesial formation, ecclesial preservation, and ecclesial
mission—that is, to enable the church to *realize* its ecclesial
essence, to be a community of faith, hope, and love, a sign and
sacrament of the kingdom of God.[2] Since in its essence the church
is a theological reality having to do with God's redemptive shaping
of human community, the task of ministry is profoundly theological. Above all else, the minister is a theologian, and the theological
purpose of ministry—to enable the church to be church—should
infuse and transform everything the minister does, whether in
pastoral care, liturgy and preaching, institutional management,
education, or social mission. The church is indeed a "treasure in
earthen vessels."[3] It is all too easy for the minister to become
preoccupied with the vessel, to forget that the treasure must infuse
and transform the vessel. The treasure without the vessel is
dissipated in formless ways; the vessel without the treasure is
merely an empty container. In order for the minister to be a
theologian, to recognize the treasure and know how to work with it,
she or he must engage in an ongoing process of theological
reflection and study. Nothing should be more central to the work of
ministry, yet nothing is more commonly neglected.

3. The fundamental role of ministry is that of leadership
—leadership in the community of Jesus Christ.[4] Rarely is it noted
that the words "priest" and "presbyter" derive from an Indo-
European root similar to the Sanskrit *purugava,* meaning "guide"
or "leader." (A presbyter is an "elder," but the essential function of
an elder, which is not dependent on one's physical age, is to guide

or lead.) This was the original and most fundamental function of ministry; only later did sacerdotal, substitutionary, hierarchical functions accrue to the office. What authorizes ministry is not the possession of jurisdiction, office, consecration, or special "call"[5] but rather the possession of knowledge, skill, and commitment. Ordination is basically a matter of recognizing and certifying the possession of such knowledge, skill, and commitment. It does not confer sacral power or authority, and it should not lead to a separate clergy class.

I am proposing a democratic-participative-secular model of ministerial office as distinguished from a hierarchical-authoritarian-sacerdotal model. Not only is this model closer to the practice of the early church, as numerous studies have shown,[6] but it is also required by the new paradigm. The minister as leader should empower the common ministry of the whole people. True leadership is not simply management or administration, and it cannot be accomplished through the application of management skills. Ministerial leadership involves at bottom articulating a vision of what the church is, of its essential being and purpose, and enabling this vision to become a productive ideal that infuses all church activities and all participants. Above all, true leadership is the antithesis of clericalism, which Ruether defines as the "separation of ministry from mutual interaction with community and its transformation into hierarchically ordered castes of clergy and laity."[7]

"Ministry" means service, ministration, *diakonia*. We could also speak of ministerial leadership as the leadership of *nurture*. In a famous book on religious education, *Christian Nurture,* published in 1861, Horace Bushnell claimed that becoming a Christian is a matter not of sudden, dramatic conversion but of a lifelong process. In a striking choice of images, he observed that there is a difference between the "ostrich nurture" (Lam. 4:3: "The daughter of my people has become cruel, like the ostriches in the wilderness"), which is "nature's type of all unmotherhood," and the "nurture and admonition of the Lord" (Eph. 6:4). "There is then," writes Bushnell, "some kind of nurture which is of the Lord, deriving a quality and power from him, and communicating the same." It is the "Lord's way of education."[8] It is also the Lord's way of ministry—a way of ministry that derives a quality and power from God. Nurture is notably a feminine image: its linguistic roots all mean to nourish, feed, suckle; and "nurture" has the same sense as the Greek word *paideia* (of which it is the translation in Eph. 6:4), namely, to rear, foster, lead, and educate a child. Nurture is an image of gentle strength, of demanding work and joyous sharing. By adopting this image and using it to suggest, in the following theses, three "nurturing" functions of ministry in the new paradigm, I am intimating that ministry has certain feminine qualities that have been deeply suppressed by the tradition but that now may be seen to be attracting women as well as men to this vocation and that have the potential of giving new life to it.

4. The minister is a nurturer of interpretive and transformative appropriations of Christian texts in light of the contemporary situation. The resources of the tradition for redemptive transformation are enormously rich. But they must be interpreted, used critically, appropriated in what Paul Ricoeur calls a "second naiveté."[9] A relationship of immediacy, or first naiveté, to Scripture and tradition is no longer feasible once people have been exposed to historical consciousness and modern science. (It is of course possible to "forget" this exposure when it comes to religion and thus to live in two worlds, one precritical and mythical, the other scientific and secular.) In a postcritical context, the power and meaning of texts can be released *only* through interpretation, but they *can* indeed be released very powerfully in this way. For example, the Genesis account of creation and fall is demonstrably false if read as a literal, scientific description of origins, but it offers profound religious insight into the relationship of God and the world and into the perplexities of finitude, knowledge, and good and evil if interpreted metaphorically or poetically.

The ecclesial tradition includes a great deal more than the Hebrew and Christian Scriptures. These are undoubtedly the norm, the classic, the center; but it would be an impoverishment to insist that they are the whole and sacrosanct. Protestant preaching has almost always been based solely on biblical texts, but it is not self-evident why this should be the case, why it should be deemed inappropriate to draw upon texts from the great postbiblical tradition, which has its own classics, along with the scriptural texts. Even churches that are relatively sophisticated in the study of Scripture generally share a vast ignorance of Christian theology throughout the history of the church. How many people, really, know anything about Origen and Augustine, Anselm and Thomas Aquinas, Luther and Calvin, Edwards and Bushnell, Schleiermacher and Kierkegaard, Barth and Tillich, Rahner and Gutiérrez, Ruether and Cone? This is a great impoverishment. Of course, there is no "canon" of tradition, at least for Protestants, but canonical status finally does not resolve anything with respect to the meaning and truth of biblical texts either. There is no avoiding the risk, the conflict, and the interplay of interpretations. Truth is strong, and it will win out in such a process. Part of the hard work of ministry is to guide and nurture the interpretive process. There is in fact a hunger among people for genuine learning and instruction, and a willingness to go much further than is generally thought possible. The problem is in part a lack of leadership, an inability to conceive and construct a total educational program in which every facet of congregational life becomes an appropriation and reconfiguration of the tradition.

5. The minister is a nurturer of a dialectic between Eucharist and human solidarity,[10] between sacrament and service, spirituality and liberation, liturgy and life, caring and justice. Here we are concerned with the praxis of the church, its action as distinguished from its reflection—a multifaceted praxis encompassing personal healing and piety, eucharistic and liturgical celebration, and world-transforming mission. This praxis must be seen as a whole; alienation occurs when it is fragmented. Many of our congregational and individual problems stem from this fragmentation: personal crises are often related to a loss of meaningful context, of objective purpose in life; Eucharist without human solidarity is an empty gesture; praxis without spiritual purpose is ideology. The minister's role is to nurture a wholeness of vision in which these things fit together in a productive way. Most middle-class Christians think of social ministry in terms of works of charity or philanthropy rather than in terms of systemic change or structural reform. It is of course both—a matter of both love and justice, of both responding to immediate, concrete needs and working for long-term reforms. But it is all too easy (because less threatening) to concentrate on the former while forgetting the latter. Most congregations—most of us!—could benefit from a good deal of consciousness-raising with respect to the facts of social injustice, structural oppression, racism, sexism, and classism. We must come to see these evils as part of the totality of sin, and to see their combating as related to the confession of faith in God—for to know God *is* to do justice. This too is part of the hard work of ministry.

6. The minister is a nurturer of ecumenical and world openness. The fundamental thrust of Christian faith is beyond provincialism in all its forms and toward a universal community of redemption. Everything culture-specific in Christianity is relativized without being discarded. We have the universal and the divine only in and

through the particular, but the particular is not an ultimate end in itself: it is the bearer of, and points beyond itself to, the universal. The work of ministry faces several sets of problems at this point, among them the need to challenge local, regional, and denominational parochialism. Because of limited experience, people tend to think that the way they do things is the best or only way, that what they believe is alone right and true. It is all too easy to be absorbed by what is familiar and ready to hand. Horizons need to be opened up, stretched, expanded. The fact of the matter is that distinctive denominational or confessional traditions are not very relevant in today's world. The real issues cut across the traditions and are not much illuminated by them—issues such as the credibility of belief in God, the meaning of Jesus' death and resurrection, the nature of human sin, the threat of nuclear holocaust, the perplexities of personal crisis, and the shock of massive poverty.

Ministerial nurture requires helping people come to terms with two further facts. The first is that Christianity is a world religion, largely non-Protestant, increasingly non-Western, encompassing a great variety of cultures and traditions, with enormous potential for both good and ill. The second is that Christianity is only one of the great religious and ethical systems of humanity, that it cannot expect to evangelize or prevail over the others, that all claims to superiority are parochial, that the survival of all may depend on finding new bases for spiritual unity that transcend anything we now know. Helping people appreciate this twofold recognition is part of the very process of deepening ourselves in the truth and validity of our own faith, and it is one of the severest, noblest works of ministry.

Epilogue.
Ecclesia
of Freedom

——————————————————— In this book we have re-
flected upon a variety of topics: the relationship of Jesus to the new
community of faith that gathered in his name; the meaning of the
terms "ecclesia" and "church"; biblical images of the church;
traditional marks or dimensions of the church (both Catholic and
Protestant); the distinction between church and sect; our contemporary cultural situation as we enter the period of "post-
modernity"; contemporary ecclesiology as it relates to what we
have called the new paradigm (including the questions of ecclesial "essence" and ecclesial "sociality," of new configurations of
the church in the liberation theologies, of the necessity of an
ecumenical world vision); and finally, the elements of a theology of
ministry as they are shaped by an emerging picture of what the
church essentially is. The several features of this picture have not
yet, however, been drawn together into a more precisely delineated
and concrete proposal. In this Epilogue, I shall make that attempt. I
offer a theological "definition" of the church in the new paradigm
which integrates the various strands of the analysis into an
encompassing vision of the ecclesial community as an ecclesia of
freedom:

> Ecclesia is a transfigured mode of human community, an image of
> the realm and rule of God embodied in a diversity of historical
> churches, comprising a plurality of peoples and cultural traditions,
> founded upon the life, death, and resurrection of Christ, created by
> the redemptive presence of God as Spirit. It is a community in which
> privatistic, provincial, and hierarchical modes of existence are
> challenged and are being overcome, and in which is fragmentarily

actualized a universal reconciling love that liberates from sin and death, alienation and oppression.

Several features of this definition relate to issues discussed in the preceding pages.

Ecclesia as both divine gift and human activity. According to the definition, ecclesia is an anticipatory sign and sacrament of the realm or kingdom or rule of God—the basileia vision of Jesus, the vision of a new realm brought into being by God's saving and transformative rule, the productive ideal of a new way of being communally human in the world and before God, a liberated communion of free subjects, a realm of freedom imaged in the ecclesia of freedom. This productive ideal, I have suggested, works within history as a power—not a causal power but a creative, luring, persuading power that creates new life and actualizes redemption in a variety of historical forms, social and individual. But this ideal transcends history precisely as it works within history. It cannot be identified with an actual or a future state of affairs; it can only be "anticipated," never grasped or finished.

When the actualization of redemption occurs in and through the historical churches, what we find is the ecclesia, which is a determinate form of the basileia—the shape it takes when faith in Jesus as the Christ and the relationship to the life, death, and resurrection of Jesus are explicit and establish the specific contours of redemption. Ecclesia thus understood is a mediating or spiritual reality; it participates in both the ideality of the basileia and the reality of the historical churches. It does not exist as an entity beside the churches but is their inner essence and telos, the source of everything that makes them churches. As a mediating, spiritual reality, ecclesia is unambiguous but fragmentary: it participates in the saving power of the basileia (God's world-transforming redemptive rule), disclosing it unambiguously but actualizing it only fragmentarily, because the instruments of actualization are historical and finite.

As a critical principle, ecclesia is unambiguous; as a practical principle, fragmentary. Hence the definition says that distorted modes of existence "are challenged and are being overcome" in the ecclesial community; in it, liberating love is truly envisioned but only "fragmentarily actualized." In brief, ecclesia links together basileia vision and real churches: without their ecclesial essence, the churches would be merely human, social institutions; and without the ecclesial community, God's redemptive, liberating power would become historically actual only in diffused, anonymous forms. The definition attempts to show this linkage and thus addresses what I have claimed is the central *theological* issue at stake for an ecclesiology in the new paradigm, namely, how the church is to be understood as both a divine gift and a human activity, both a spirit-filled community and a historical institution.

Ecclesia as people, body, communion, Spirit. The definition incorporates the biblical images that were analyzed in chapter 1—people, body, communion, Spirit—allowing these ancient symbols to help establish the main lineaments of a new ecclesiology. Ecclesia is the people of God, one people yet drawn from a plurality of peoples and cultural traditions. It is the body whose unique intersubjectivity is shaped by the life, death, and resurrection of Christ. It is a transfigured mode of human community, a koinonia of faith, hope, and love. And its source of vitality is the creative, upbuilding work of the Spirit of God. Much of the substance of what has been said about ecclesiology in the latter part of the work was anticipated by the discussion of the biblical images in the first part: the new paradigm has been born out of the old, and in it the tradition is both deconstructed and reconstructed.

Ecclesia as one, holy, catholic, and apostolic. The definition also incorporates the classic doctrinal marks of the church—one, holy, catholic, apostolic—while attempting to reformulate them in light of new expectations. The church's unity is fashioned out of plurality and seeks the common ground not only of Christian faith but of the many human modes of apprehending the holy. Its catholicity, its inner wholeness or integrity, resides in its overcoming privatistic, provincial, and hierarchical modes of existence and in its orientation to the universal redemption of humanity. Its holiness consists in its ecclesial essence as a liberated communion of free subjects under the grace of God; it exists *sola gratia* (by grace alone), but is a *communio peccatorum* (communion of sinners) as well as a *communio sanctorum* (communion of saints). And its apostolicity takes the form of witness to Christ and mission in his name; it exists *sola Christus* (by Christ alone), but its mission, its apostolic mission, entails service in and to the world and a sharing in common struggles against dehumanization, alienation, and oppression.

Ecclesia as liberating and ecumenical. The definition responds to the expectations of the new paradigm. The first of these was discussed in calling the church both divine gift and human activity. It is the need to work out a contemporary theological understanding of the church as a spiritual, historical, and social community. Beyond this, and above all, I am attempting to understand this community in terms oriented to the praxis of liberation. Ecclesial community is human community transfigured in the direction of liberation—liberation through Christ from all provincialisms and oppressions based on race, sex, class, dogma, ideology, location, culture, and so on; liberation from personal and social forms of sin, from the burdens of law and guilty conscience, from the ultimate emptiness and alienation of death. Freedom is the critical mark of ecclesia in our time. The definition hints finally at the ecumenical, global context by suggesting that the ecclesial community encompasses a plurality of peoples and cultural traditions and is but one of several religiocultural shapes assumed by what Christians call the kingdom of God but what other religions give other names.

It should be clear that this definition with its particular way of retrieving and integrating the images and marks of the church reflects the ecumenical, liberative, and critical exigencies of our time. In this respect, it is a contingent, relative definition that has no pretense of being perennially valid.

Ecclesia as critical principle of praxis. Of course, no actual church adequately embodies the elements of the definition, but when an actual church asks itself what it ought to be, it cannot avoid reflecting upon itself in some such fashion as this unless it is willing to give up the question of its essential being. Without the discipline of critical self-reflection, the church would succumb to its persistent tendency to lose its ecclesial essence—to drift into becoming a privatistic, alienated, merely human association serving certain social functions such as the disburdening of individuals and the maintenance of authority structures. We know all too well that churches can fail miserably as ecclesial communities, can in fact become positively antiecclesial. It is all the more important, therefore, to be able to specify what the essential and constitutive features of ecclesia are, in order to have a critical principle against which these distortions can be measured.

Of course no definition can of itself combat the distortions. If we were to remain at the stage of definition, the definition itself would be falsified: the church must become in praxis what it understands itself to be in essence, and often it only discovers in praxis what it ought to be in essence. True praxis requires a critical theory, and a critical theory is only a theory of praxis. By entering into praxis, we are entering into the realm of historical struggle, conflict, and compromise. An abstract or rigid idealism at this point does no good at all. The very purpose of having a productive or practical ideal such as that of the ecclesia of freedom is to realize it in historical forms. Such an ideal can in fact be a tremendously powerful factor in the historical process. Although this process is an ongoing one, requiring constant vigilance and a recognition that all historical realizations of ecclesial freedom are incomplete, we are encouraged in our work of realization by the confidence Paul gives us that "the creation itself will be set free from its bondage to decay and obtain the glorious liberty of the children of God" (Rom. 8:21).

Notes

INTRODUCTION: WHAT IS THE NEW PARADIGM?

1. See Gustavo Gutiérrez, *The Power of the Poor in History* (Maryknoll, N.Y.: Orbis Books, 1983), chaps. 7 and 8. Gutiérrez's expression "theology from the underside of history" was suggested by Dietrich Bonhoeffer (see *Power of the Poor,* 231).

2. Such is the proposal of Langdon Gilkey in "The New Watershed in Theology," in *Society and the Sacred: Toward a Theology of Culture in Decline* (New York: Crossroad, 1981), 3–14. See also his "Events, Meanings, and the Current Tasks of Theology," *Journal of the American Academy of Religion* 53 (1985): 717–34. I rely heavily in the following pages on Gilkey's analyses of the current cultural situation.

3. See Thomas Kuhn, *The Structure of Scientific Revolutions,* 2d ed. (Chicago: Univ. of Chicago Press, 1970), esp. 150.

4. For a good summary of the impact of the Enlightenment on theology, see Robert King's analysis in *Christian Theology: An Introduction to Its Traditions and Tasks,* ed. Peter C. Hodgson and Robert H. King, 2d ed. (Philadelphia: Fortress Press, 1985), 10–12. King summarizes the classical theological consensus on pp. 2–10.

5. Gilkey, *Society and the Sacred,* 6.

6. Mark C. Taylor, *Erring: A Postmodern A/theology* (Chicago: Univ. of Chicago Press, 1984), esp. 3–18.

7. Gilkey, *Society and the Sacred,* 8.

8. The French biologist Jacques Monod appropriates the famous words of Democritus for the title of his book *Chance and Necessity: An Essay on the Natural Philosophy of Modern Biology* (New York: Vintage Books, 1972).

9. Gilkey points all this out quite effectively, in *Society and the Sacred,* 6–7.

10. Lee Cormie provides an excellent analysis of these matters in "Liberation and Salvation: A First World View," in *The Challenge of Liberation Theology: A First World Response,* ed. L. Dale Richesin and Brian Mahan (Maryknoll, N.Y.: Orbis Books, 1981), 21–47. See also Juan

Luis Segundo, *Faith and Ideologies,* trans. John Drury (Maryknoll, N.Y.: Orbis Books, 1984), esp. chap. 10.

11. Gilkey, *Society and the Sacred,* 12.

12. See John Cobb, *Beyond Dialogue: Toward a Mutual Transformation of Christianity and Buddhism* (Philadelphia: Fortress Press, 1982). The best recent discussion is provided by Paul F. Knitter, in *No Other Name? A Critical Survey of Christian Attitudes toward the World Religions* (Maryknoll, N.Y.: Orbis Books, 1985).

13. Taylor, *Erring,* 6.

14. Frank Lentricchia has pointed this out in *After the New Criticism* (Chicago: Univ. of Chicago Press, 1980), 168–88.

15. Gilkey has analyzed these two extremes at some length in "Events, Meanings, and the Current Tasks of Theology," 718–28.

16. *Aufhebung* is the key to all of Hegel's logical and historical transitions. See Charles Taylor, *Hegel* (Cambridge: Cambridge Univ. Press, 1975), esp. 119. On preserving the historical and sensible by "letting it pass away," see G. W. F. Hegel, *Lectures on the Philosophy of Religion,* ed. and trans. P. C. Hodgson et al., vol. 3 (Berkeley and Los Angeles: Univ. of California Press, 1985), 222.

17. Ernst Troeltsch stressed the necessity of having the courage to act in situations of objective and intellectual uncertainty, for action can clarify, can help to resolve things slowly, when theoretical questions remain irresolvable. He also called for the creation of a new synthesis of cultural values in the wake of the crisis of Western culture brought about by the First World War. His prophetic words went unheeded, and he died before he could contribute to their realization. See his *Christian Thought: Its History and Application,* ed. Baron F. von Hügel (London: Univ. of London Press, 1923), esp. 69–129. The call for a new cultural and theological paradigm involves taking up Troeltsch's agenda again some seventy years later.

1. ELEMENTS OF THE CHURCH IN THE CLASSIC PARADIGM

1. See Oscar Cullman, *Peter: Disciple, Apostle, Martyr: A Historical and Theological Essay,* trans. Floyd V. Filson (Philadelphia: Westminster Press, 1953); Hans Küng, *The Church* (New York: Image Books, 1976), 103–14; and Francis Schüssler Fiorenza, *Foundational Theology: Jesus and the Church* (New York: Crossroad, 1984), chap. 3.

2. The term *basileia* is generally translated as "kingdom" or "reign," and the image is certainly that of royal dominion, the rule of a king over his territory or people. It presupposes the royal metaphors for God that abound in Hebrew Scripture, metaphors that are both hierarchical and patriarchal, and for that reason the image has become problematic for us. But Jesus transformed this imagery by his parabolic appropriation of it; the vision of a "new world" evoked by the parables is anything but hierarchical and patriarchal. We propose to think of the basileia in terms of images of "world" or "realm" (the latter still has regal overtones) rather than of "kingdom" and "dominion." Augustine's expression *civitas Dei,* "city of God," is perhaps the best choice of all. Normally, however, I simply

use the Greek term *basileia* without translating it, intending that its meaning be filled out through its usage.

3. Fiorenza, *Foundational Theology,* 134. See also Dorothee Soelle, *Political Theology,* trans. John Shelley (Philadelphia: Fortress Press, 1974), 64–67.

4. John Knox, *The Church and the Reality of Christ* (New York: Harper & Row, 1962), 23–24.

5. Edward Farley has made this point. See his *Ecclesial Reflection: An Anatomy of Theological Method* (Philadelphia: Fortress Press, 1982), 18–25; see also Edward Farley and Peter C. Hodgson, "Scripture and Tradition," in *Christian Theology: An Introduction to Its Traditions and Tasks,* ed. Peter C. Hodgson and Robert H. King, 2d ed. (Philadelphia: Fortress Press, 1985), 67–68.

6. I return to these theological considerations on the origin of the church and provide historical evidence supporting them when we take up feminist views of the church and esp. the work of Elisabeth Schüssler Fiorenza, in chap. 2 below.

7. Thus K. L. Schmidt, in *Theological Dictionary of the New Testament (TDNT),* ed. Gerhard Kittel, trans. Geoffrey W. Bromiley, vol. 3 (Grand Rapids: Wm. B. Eerdmans, 1965), 531.

8. On the Greek and Septuagint usage, see *TDNT* 3:527–29; *Die Religion in Geschichte und Gegenwart (RGG),* 3d ed., vol. 3 (Tübingen: J. C. B. Mohr [Paul Siebeck], 1959), cols. 1297–98; and Eric G. Jay, *The Church: Its Changing Image through Twenty Centuries,* 2 vols. (Richmond: John Knox Press, 1980; London: SPCK, 1977), 1:5–7. The Hellenistic Jewish usage has been the subject of more recent scholarship, summarized in Fiorenza's *Foundational Theology,* 126. Fiorenza refers especially to the work of Klaus Berger, Günther Bornkamm, and Lucien Cerfaux.

9. I am indebted to Fernando Segovia for these observations, which he made in a lecture to the class at Vanderbilt on the nature of the church and its ministries. Segovia points to the irony in the fact that the inclusiveness of the early community did not extend to Judaism itself. The anti-Judaic polemic that is present esp. in the Matthean and Johannine traditions suggests that the community that was excluded by Judaism itself soon became exclusive. The falling-away from the radical meaning of the gospel presaged the reappearance of patriarchal, hierarchical, and sacerdotal patterns as well.

10. See *RGG* 3:1299, and *TDNT* 3:504–12.

11. See *TDNT* 3:515; *RGG* 3:1304; and Küng, *The Church,* 117.

12. This is Edward Farley's proposal. See his *Ecclesial Reflection,* 205; see also Farley and Hodgson, "Scripture and Tradition," 62–63.

13. *TDNT* 3:516.

14. Paul Minear, *Images of the Church in the New Testament* (Philadelphia: Westminster Press, 1960). See the summary lists of images on pp. 268–69.

15. The following discussion draws upon helpful analyses contained in Küng's *The Church,* sec. C; Jay's *The Church,* chap. 2; Minear's *Images,* chaps. 3–6; as well as in the appropriate articles in *TDNT* and *RGG.* The interpretive thesis, however, is my own, and much of the exegetical study is

original. The discussion of the relationship of ecclesia and basileia is reserved for the next section.

16. Jay, *The Church* 1:30.

17. In this I am following Eduard Schweizer, *The Church as the Body of Christ* (Richmond: John Knox Press, 1964), chaps. 2–4.

18. For an elaboration of a theology of resurrection along these lines, see my *Jesus—Word and Presence: An Essay in Christology* (Philadelphia: Fortress Press, 1971), chap. 5.

19. The following survey is indebted to information provided by Jay in *The Church* 1:30, 50, 64, 77–81, 84–85, 102–3, 107, 110, 114–18, 133, 140, 150–51, 171, 174.

20. Our word "fellowship" comes from an Anglo-Saxon root meaning the laying down of money or property for a joint undertaking; one who does that is a "fellow," a "fee layer." The word does not have a masculine referent and is not sex-specific. "Communion" has the root sense of mutual "building" and thus is directly associated with the "building" work of the Spirit, as we shall see.

21. See Jay, *The Church* 1:85, 104, 119, 131.

22. I shall return to these images when discussing the "spirituality" and "historicality" of the church under the rubric of "ecclesial essence" in chap. 2 below. The expressions "community of the Spirit" or "spiritual community" and "God existing as community" derive from Hegel. See G. W. F. Hegel, *Lectures on the Philosophy of Religion*, ed. and trans. P. C. Hodgson et al., vol. 3 (Berkeley and Los Angeles: Univ. of California Press, 1985), 140–42, 328–31. The expression "spiritual community" was taken over and developed by Paul Tillich, in *Systematic Theology*, vol. 3 (Chicago: Univ. of Chicago Press, 1963), 111–245. Dietrich Bonhoeffer adopted the first expression and modified the second ("Christ existing as the church"); see his *The Communion of Saints: A Dogmatic Inquiry into the Sociology of the Church* (New York: Harper & Row, 1963), 134, 146–47.

23. See Jay, *The Church* 1:30–31, 54, 79, 85–87, 118.

24. See Yves Congar, *The Mystery of the Church*, trans. A. V. Littledale (Baltimore: Helicon Press, 1960), 100–104. I shall discuss Thomas's ecclesiology in more detail below under the theme of "holiness."

25. See Hans Küng's excellent discussion, in "The Church as the Creation of the Spirit," in *The Church*, 215–36.

26. On our reasons for normally not translating this term, see n. 2 of the present chap.

27. Küng makes this point repeatedly, in *The Church*, 124–44.

28. I am indebted to Francis Fiorenza for this term and the following remarks. See his *Foundational Theology*, 117, 134–35.

29. See chap. 2 below, on "ecclesial essence."

30. Among the first were John of Ragusa's *Tractatus de Ecclesia* (1431), directed against Hus; and Juan de Torquemada's *Summa de Ecclesia* (1486), subsequently used against the Reformers. See Küng, *The Church*, 345.

31. "Pisteuomen . . . eis mian, hagian, katholikēn kai apostolikēn ekklēsian." This phrase is not found in the Nicene Creed of 325. In the text of the Apostles' Creed, the "in," *eis,* of belief is not repeated before "holy

catholic church." The Latin text reads, "Credo in Spiritum Sanctum; sanctam ecclesiam catholicam . . . " ("I believe in the Holy Spirit; [I believe] the holy catholic church . . ."). Strictly speaking, one believes *in* only God, Christ, and the Spirit. The earliest versions of the Apostles' Creed, like the Nicene Creed, made no mention of the church at all. When reference to the church first appeared, in the creed of Cyprian of Carthage (250), it read, "I believe . . . in the Holy Spirit. I believe the forgiveness of sins and eternal life through [*per*] the holy church." The familiar version of this portion of the Apostles' Creed was established by the 4th cent., although the adjective "catholic" was not added until the 5th cent. See Philip Schaff, *The Creeds of Christendom,* vol. 2 (New York: Harper & Bros., 1890), 20, 45, 52–55, 57–58, 60. It appears, then, that when reference to the church was added to the creeds, the church was first viewed as an instrumentality of belief, the place where the Spirit is at work; then it was to be "believed" (along with the forgiveness of sin, the resurrection of the body, the life everlasting, etc.) but not "believed in" in the sense that God is to be believed in. But eventually the church itself became an object of belief in the full sense, as the text of the Niceno-Constantinopolitan Creed testifies.

32. I am indebted to Küng's rich discussion in "Dimensions of the Church," in sec. D. of *The Church.* Much valuable historical information is provided by Jay, in *The Church,* as well as by the compact summaries of the history of the doctrine of the church in *RGG* (3d ed.), 3:1304–11; and in *The New Schaff-Herzog Encyclopedia of Religious Knowledge,* ed. Samuel Macauley Jackson (New York: Funk and Wagnalls Co., 1908–), 3:79–84.

33. Quoted in Jay's *The Church* 1:67–68; cf. chap. 5.

34. I am indebted to my colleague Jean Porter for these remarks.

35. Jay, *The Church* 1:86–87.

36. Küng, *The Church,* 383–86. On the historical matters discussed in this paragraph and the next, see also Jay, *The Church* 1:44, 68, 73, 76, 89–90; and *RGG* 3:1307.

37. Küng, *The Church,* 391. It is not a little ironic that when, upon the insistence of the Vatican, Küng was stripped of his appointment as professor of Catholic theology at the University of Tübingen, he retained the position of professor of ecumenical theology. The latter was an appointment of the state and not subject to the concordat with the Vatican.

38. Ibid., 389–90; and Jürgen Moltmann, *The Church in the Power of the Spirit: A Contribution to Messianic Ecclesiology,* trans. Margaret Kohl (New York: Harper & Row, 1977), 337–52.

39. For the historical information contained in these two paragraphs, see Jay, *The Church* 1:53–56, 59–64, 81–82, 88.

40. Congar, *Mystery of the Church,* 99–103; and Thomas Aquinas, *Theological Texts,* ed. Thomas Gilby (London: Oxford Univ. Press), 341.

41. See Bonhoeffer, *Communion of Saints,* 86, 146–47.

42. Küng, *The Church,* 443–55.

43. Ibid., 456–59, 563–64 (although Küng wants to think of this as an apostolic succession).

44. See Geddes MacGregor, *Corpus Christi: The Nature of the Church according to the Reformed Tradition* (Philadelphia: Westminster Press, 1958), 5.

45. See Küng, *The Church*, 361–64.
46. Dale Johnson has impressed this on me by a lecture comparing several Protestant ecclesiologies.
47. For the following, I rely primarily on Jay, *The Church*, 1:162–65, 170–71; and MacGregor, *Corpus Christi*, 8–10, 20–21, 41–42, 45–47, 49–56.
48. In *Luther's Works*, ed. J. Pelikan and H. T. Lehmann, vol. 39, ed. Eric W. Gritsch (Philadelphia: Fortress Press, 1970), 55–104, esp. 65, 69–70.
49. Luther's version of the Creed, "Credo in Spiritum Sanctum, sanctorum communionem," omits the intervening phrase, *sanctam ecclesiam catholicam.* As we have seen, Luther disliked the word "church," *Kirche,* and preferred terms such as "community," *Gemeinde,* "congregation," *Gemeine,* and "assembly," *Sammlung,* as translations of the Greek *ekklēsia.*
50. Ferdinand Christian Baur, *The Epochs of Church Historiography* (1852), chap. 7, secs. 1–3; in *Ferdinand Christian Baur on the Writing of Church History,* ed. and trans. P. C. Hodgson (New York: Oxford Univ. Press, 1968), 241–53.
51. Paul Tillich, "The Protestant Principle and the Proletarian Situation," in *The Protestant Era,* trans. James Luther Adams (Chicago: Univ. of Chicago Press, 1948), 163. Such "protest" is intrinsic to the meaning of "protestant" in Tillich's view.
52. See Paul Tillich, *Systematic Theology* 3:243–45.
53. Ernst Troeltsch, *The Social Teaching of the Christian Churches,* trans. Olive Wyon, 2 vols. (London: George Allen & Unwin, 1931), 1:331–43; and idem, "Kirche: III. Dogmatisch," in *Die Religion in Geschichte und Gegenwart,* 1st ed. (Tübingen: J. C. B. Mohr [Paul Siebeck], 1909), 3:1147–55. For this typology, Troeltsch was guided by the sociological categories of Max Weber.
54. Troeltsch, *Social Teaching* 1:342 (trans. slightly altered).
55. Ernst Troeltsch, in *RGG* (1st ed.), 3:1152–53.
56. Ibid. 3:1153–55.

2. TOWARD A THEOLOGY OF THE CHURCH IN THE NEW PARADIGM

1. Leonardo Boff, *Ecclesiogenesis: The Base Communities Reinvent the Church,* trans. Robert R. Barr (Maryknoll, N.Y.: Orbis Books, 1986).
2. In the categorial scheme of German idealism, the terms "essence" and "idea" are closely related. According to Hegel's *Logic,* essence is the ground of existence and must appear, take on actuality, be active. Similarly, "idea" is the unity of "concept" and "objectivity," containing within itself the impulse to go forth into the real (G. W. F. Hegel, *Encyclopedia of the Philosophical Sciences,* part 1, *The Science of Logic,* trans. William Wallace [Oxford: Oxford Univ. Press, 1892],§§ 112, 213). I cannot discuss the technicalities here but simply point out that in English the word "essence" lends itself better to our intended meaning than the word "idea."
3. Among the others I should want to include, on the Protestant side, F.

C. Baur, Horace Bushnell, Josiah Royce, Karl Barth, Dietrich Bonhoeffer, Langdon Gilkey, Claude Welch, Jürgen Moltmann, Wolfhart Pannenberg; on the Catholic side, the Tübingen school of 19th-cent. Catholicism (J. S. Drey, J. A. Möhler), the French *nouvelle théologie* of the 20th cent. (Emile Mersch, Henri de Lubac, Yves Congar), several post-Vatican II theologians (Bernard Lonergan, Karl Rahner, J. B. Metz, Edward Schillebeeckx, Hans Küng, Bernard Cooke); and among Anglicans, S. T. Coleridge, J. H. Newman and the Oxford Movement, F. D. Maurice, and Lionel Thornton. Not all these have worked on ecclesiology in the strict sense, but they have contributed to the problematic with which I am here concerned.

4. See Trutz Rendtorff, *Church and Theology: The Systematic Function of the Church Concept in Modern Theology* (Philadelphia: Westminster Press, 1962), esp. chap. 2.

5. Friedrich Schleiermacher, *The Christian Faith,* ed. H. R. Macintosh and J. S. Stewart (Edinburgh: T. & T. Clark, 1928). References in the text are to the sec. nos. of the 2d Germ. ed.

6. G. W. F. Hegel, *Lectures on the Philosophy of Religion,* ed. and trans. P. C. Hodgson et al., vol. 3, *The Consummate Religion* (Berkeley and Los Angeles: Univ. of California Press, 1985), 133–62, 223–47, 328–47; see esp. 135–42, 328–33, 339–42.

7. Ernst Troeltsch, "What Does 'Essence of Christianity' Mean?" (1903, 1913), in *Writings on Theology and Religion,* ed. and trans. Robert Morgan and Michael Pye (London: Gerald Duckworth & Co., 1977), 124–81.

8. The foundation for this theory is found in Troeltsch's philosophy of history. See his *Gesammelte Schriften,* vol. 3, *Der Historismus und seine Probleme* (Tübingen: J. C. B. Mohr [Paul Siebeck], 1922), chap. 2. A less technical summary of elements of the theory is found in Troeltsch's *Christian Thought: Its History and Application,* ed. Baron F. von Hügel (London: Univ. of London Press, 1923), sec. 3, "Ethics and the Philosophy of History."

9. Troeltsch, *Writings,* 154.

10. See Troeltsch, *Christian Thought,* 32–35; idem, *Der Historismus und seine Probleme,* 183–86; and idem, *Glaubenslehre* (Munich and Leipzig: Duncker & Humblot, 1925), part 2, chap. 1.

11. H. Richard Niebuhr (in collaboration with Daniel Day Williams and James M. Gustafson), *The Purpose of the Church and Its Ministry: Reflections on the Aims of Theological Education* (New York: Harper & Bros., 1956), 17–27.

12. Ibid., 31, 39–47.

13. Paul Tillich, *Systematic Theology,* vol. 3, *Life and the Spirit: History and the Kingdom of God* (Chicago: Univ. of Chicago Press, 1963), part 4, chaps. 2–3). For the following analysis, see esp. pp. 107–10, 138–40, 149–61, 162–82, 243–45.

14. We may also, to be sure, think of a transhistorical consummation —the end of the temporal-historical process, and the end of the individual person—for which, in my view, the symbol of "eternal life" is more appropriate than that of "kingdom of God."

15. Hegel, *Lectures on the Philosophy of Religion* 3:140.

16. Hegel, *Encyclopedia of the Philosophical Sciences,* trans. from the 3d

Germ. ed. W. Wallace and A. V. Miller, part 3, *Hegel's Philosophy of Mind* (Oxford: Clarendon Press, 1971),§ 381.

17. Cf. Hegel, *Lectures on the Philosophy of Religion,* vol. 1, *Introduction and The Concept of Religion* (Berkeley and Los Angeles: Univ. of California Press, 1984), 325.

18. Langdon Gilkey has pointed this out in *How the Church Can Minister to the World without Losing Itself* (New York: Harper & Row, 1964), chaps. 1 and 2. For a somewhat similar analysis of the situation in present-day Germany, see J. B. Metz, *The Emergent Church: The Future of Christianity in a Postbourgeois World* (New York: Crossroad, 1981), esp. chap. 4.

19. This summary is from Howard Harrod's lectures to the course at Vanderbilt on the nature of the church and its ministries. See also James Gustafson's discussion of the church as a "natural" and a "political" community, in *Treasure in Earthen Vessels: The Church as a Human Community* (New York: Harper & Bros., 1961), chaps. 2 and 3. Harrod points out that in sociological analysis "function" does not necessarily mean "utility." Rather it refers to sets of relationships within the social world, such as in *"Y is a function of X."* The church inevitably has social functions. But how it exercises those functions and whether it allows itself simply to become a utilitarian tool is another matter, depending on specific instances and practices.

20. Gustafson, *Treasure,* chaps. 4–7.

21. Ibid., appendix. Here Gustafson discusses his theoretical dependence on Augustine, Emile Bergson, Josiah Royce, Wilhelm Dilthey, G. H. Mead, and H. R. Niebuhr.

22. Edward Farley, *Ecclesial Man: A Social Phenomenology of Faith and Reality* (Philadelphia: Fortress Press, 1975), chaps. 4–7. I have also been guided by a number of conversations with Farley.

23. Bernard Cooke (*Ministry to Word and Sacraments* [Philadelphia: Fortress Press, 1976]) adds a fourth essential function: administration and order, or what he calls ministering to God's judgment. Though it may be instrumental to the first three, it does not seem to me to have the same essential connection with the church's distinctive sociality.

24. G. W. F. Hegel, *Lectures on the Philosophy of Religion* 3:65; and idem, *Encyclopedia of the Philosophical Sciences,* part 3, *Hegel's Philosophy of Mind,* § 482. For a full elaboration of this theme, see my *New Birth of Freedom: A Theology of Bondage and Liberation* (Philadelphia: Fortress Press, 1976), upon which the following introductory paragraphs are based.

25. The famous distinction between stages of freedom—"one," "some," "all"—is that of Hegel, in *Lectures on the Philosophy of World History,* intro., *Reason in History,* trans. from the Hoffmeister ed. by H. B. Nisbet (Cambridge: Cambridge Univ. Press, 1975), 54.

26. Peter J. Paris, *The Social Teaching of the Black Churches* (Philadelphia: Fortress Press, 1985), chap. 1.

27. The following material is based on my *Children of Freedom: Black Liberation in Christian Perspective* (Philadelphia: Fortress Press, 1974). The primary historical sources on which I have relied are John Hope Franklin, *From Slavery to Freedom: A History of Negro Americans,* 3d ed.

(New York: Vintage Books, 1969); Herbert Aptheker, ed., *A Documentary History of the Negro People in the United States,* 2 vols. (New York: Citadel Press, 1951); E. Franklin Frazier, *The Negro Church in America* (New York: Schocken Books, 1963); Melville J. Herskovits, *The Myth of the Negro Past* (Boston: Beacon Press, 1958); W. E. B. Du Bois, *The Souls of Black Folk* and *The Negro Church* (both originally pub. in 1903); Benjamin Mays, *The Negro's God as Reflected in His Literature,* 2d ed. (New York: Atheneum, 1968); Howard Thurman, *The Negro Spiritual Speaks of Life and Death,* 2d ed. (New York: Harper & Row, 1969); James Cone, *The Spirituals and the Blues* (New York: Seabury Press, 1972); and Gayraud Wilmore, *Black Religion and Black Radicalism,* 2d ed. (Maryknoll, N.Y.: Orbis Books, 1983). The best and most recent study of one aspect of the subject is Albert J. Raboteau's *Slave Religion: The "Invisible Institution" in the Antebellum South* (New York: Oxford Univ. Press, 1978).

28. Frazier, *The Negro Church in America,* 16–19.

29. Frederick Douglass, *The Life and Times of Frederick Douglass* (repr. from the rev. ed. [1892]; New York: Collier Books, 1962), 151–53, 109, 112.

30. James Cone, "Sanctification, Liberation, and Black Worship," *Theology Today* 35 (1978): 139–52. See also idem, *God of the Oppressed* (New York: Seabury Press, 1975), and other recent works.

31. Frazier, *The Negro Church in America,* chap. 3.

32. A brief annotated list of the major works is given here, more or less in order of publication in English. All are pub. by Orbis Books, Maryknoll, N.Y. (the publ. house of the Catholic Foreign Mission Society of America) unless otherwise noted. Juan Luis Segundo's *The Community Called Church* (1973), the 1st vol. of his *Theology for Artisans of a New Humanity,* was written prior to the present phase of discussion, and it is not specifically oriented to the Latin American situation and the base communities; nonetheless, it is a rich theological treatise focused on the question of the "essence of the ecclesial community" (chap. 2). Gustavo Gutiérrez's *A Theology of Liberation: History, Politics, and Salvation* (1973) remains the classic work of Latin American liberation theology; the 2d part of Gutiérrez's constructive proposal is ecclesial ("The Christian Community and the New Society"). Important materials are also found in his *The Power of the Poor in History* (1983), a collection of essays from the 1970s, and in his *We Drink from Our Own Wells* (1984), which offers a spirituality of liberation. Sergio Torres and John Eagleson edited *The Challenge of Basic Christian Communities* (1981), a collection of papers from the meeting of the International Ecumenical Congress of Theology at São Paulo in 1980. Valuable factual information is also provided by Alvaro Barreiro's *Basic Ecclesial Communities: The Evangelization of the Poor* (1982). Jon Sobrino's *The True Church and the Poor* (1984) is, in my view, flawed by a degree of theological and methodological dogmatism. Leonardo Boff's *Ecclesiogenesis: The Base Communities Reinvent the Church* (1986) is undoubtedly one of the most important works on our topic, and I shall rely on it heavily along with Gutiérrez. Five of the chaps. were published in Portuguese in 1977, and the remaining two in the early eighties, but the book was not translated until Boff became a cause célèbre

as a result of the Vatican's attempt to silence him, in a controversy instigated by his more recent work, *Church—Charism and Power: Liberation Theology and the Institutional Church* (Portuguese ed., 1981; New York: Crossroad, 1985). Juan Luis Segundo has provided a no-holds-barred analysis of this controversy in *Theology and the Church: A Response to Cardinal Ratziner and a Warning to the Whole Church* (Minneapolis: Winston Press, 1985). For information on Protestant developments, see Guillermo Cook, *The Expectation of the Poor: Latin American Basic Ecclesial Communities in Protestant Perspective* (1985).

33. See Gutiérrez, *The Power of the Poor in History,* chap. 8, "The Limitations of Modern Technology: On a Letter of Dietrich Bonhoeffer." The connection between Bonhoeffer's "history of the world from beneath" (*Gesammelte Schriften,* vol. 2 [Munich: Chr. Kaiser Verlag, 1965], 441 [quoted by Gutiérrez, on p. 231]) and the "base communities" is striking. As Gutiérrez says (chap. 7), this is a "theology from the underside of history."

34. This term was introduced by Paulo Freire in *Pedagogy of the Oppressed* (New York: Herder & Herder, 1972).

35. For some information on the base communities, I am indebted to Hilquias Bezerra Cavalcanti Filho.

36. Gutiérrez, *Theology of Liberation,* chap. 12.

37. Boff, *Ecclesiogenesis,* 21.

38. Ibid., 4–9.

39. Ibid., 17–19.

40. Ibid., 15, 23–33. Boff's more explicit articulation of this critique of the hierarchical church in *Church—Charism and Power* led to his conflict with and silencing by Rome. Quite apart from the "immanentist," "secularist," and "Marxist" bogies raised by the "Instruction on Certain Aspects of 'Liberation Theology,'" issued by Cardinal Ratzinger and the Congregation for the Doctrine of the Faith in September 1984, it is clear that the real concern was the threat to hierarchical authority posed by the base communities and their theological supporters. Article 9.13 of the "Instruction" states rather baldly, "Building on such a concept of the church of the people, a critique of the very structures of the church is developed. . . . It has to do with a challenge to the sacramental and hierarchical structure of the church, which was willed by the Lord himself. . . . Theologically, this position means that ministers take their origins from the people who therefore designate ministers of their own choice in accord with the needs of their historic revolutionary mission" (quoted in Segundo's *Theology and the Church,* 182; see esp. chap. 4 of *Theology and the Church* on this matter). For a good brief analysis of the Vatican document, see Anselm Min, "The Vatican, Marxism, and Liberation Theology," *Cross Currents* 34 (1984–85): 439–55.

41. Richard Shaull has pointed out some of these connections, in *Heralds of a New Reformation: The Poor of South and North America* (Maryknoll, N.Y.: Orbis Books, 1984).

42. Gutiérrez, *Theology of Liberation,* chap. 12.

43. Ibid., 271.

44. See Sheldon B. Liss, *Marxist Thought in Latin America* (Berkeley and Los Angeles: Univ. of California Press, 1984).

45. See esp. Juan Luis Segundo, *Faith and Ideologies* (Maryknoll, N.Y.: Orbis Books, 1984), part 3; José Míguez-Bonino, *Christians and Marxists: The Mutual Challenge to Revolution* (Grand Rapids: Wm. B. Eerdmans, 1976); and Gutiérrez, *Theology of Liberation*, part 3.

46. Gutiérrez, *Power of the Poor in History*, 126; see the whole of part 3 of this book.

47. Gutiérrez, *Theology of Liberation*, 288–90; see the whole of chap. 13.

48. See esp. Gustavo Gutiérrez, *We Drink from Our Own Wells: The Spiritual Journey of a People* (Maryknoll, N.Y.: Orbis Books, 1984).

49. G. W. F. Hegel, *Phenomenology of Spirit*, trans. A. V. Miller (Oxford: Oxford Univ. Press, 1977), chap. 4.A.

50. Rosemary Radford Ruether, *To Change the World: Christology and Cultural Criticism* (New York: Crossroad, 1983), 54.

51. Ernst Troeltsch, *The Social Teaching of the Christian Churches*, trans. Olive Wyon, 2 vols. (London: George Allen & Unwin, 1931), 1:44–45.

52. I am indebted to Sallie McFague for a number of suggestions relating to this section.

53. Elisabeth Schüssler Fiorenza's major work is *In Memory of Her: A Feminist Theological Reconstruction of Christian Origins* (New York: Crossroad, 1983); see also her *Bread Not Stones: The Challenge of Feminist Biblical Interpretation* (Boston: Beacon Press, 1984) and her *Claiming the Center: A Feminist Critical Theology of Liberation* (New York: Seabury Press, 1985). Rosemary Radford Ruether's most important and recent work bearing on our subject is *Women-Church: Theology and Practice of Feminist Liturgical Communities* (San Francisco: Harper & Row, 1985); see also her *Sexism and God-Talk: Toward a Feminist Theology* (Boston: Beacon Press, 1983) and her *New Woman/New Earth: Sexist Ideologies and Human Liberation* (New York: Seabury Press, 1975). Valuable contributions have also been made by Letty M. Russell (*Human Liberation in a Feminist Perspective* [Philadelphia: Westminster Press, 1974]) and Phyllis Trible (*God and the Rhetoric of Sexuality* [Philadelphia: Fortress Press, 1978]). See also the earlier work of Sheila Collins, Georgia Harkness, Valerie Saiving, and others. Some excellent anthologies are available: Rosemary Radford Ruether, ed., *Religion and Sexism: Images of Woman in the Jewish and Christian Traditions* (New York: Simon & Schuster, 1974); Rosemary Radford Ruether and Eleanor McLaughlin, eds., *Women of Spirit: Female Leadership in the Jewish and Christian Traditions* (New York: Simon & Schuster, 1979); and Rosemary Radford Ruether, ed., *Womanguides: Readings Toward a Feminist Theology* (Boston: Beacon Press, 1985).

54. I am indebted to Jean Porter for this observation. The post-Christian feminists in whom the alienated tradition is perhaps most clearly present are Mary Daly (*Beyond God the Father* [Boston: Beacon Press, 1973]; *Gyn/Ecology: The Metaethics of Radical Feminism* [Boston: Beacon Press, 1978]; *Pure Lust: Elemental Feminist Philosophy* [Boston: Beacon Press, 1984]) and Carol P. Christ (*Women's Spiritual Quest* [Boston: Beacon Press, 1979]). Others have moved away from the Jewish tradition, such as Judith Plaskow and Naomi R. Goldenberg, and still others stand

outside the Judeo-Christian tradition entirely, such as Starhawk and Zsuzsanna E. Budapest. See part 4 of the anthology *Womanspirit Rising: A Feminist Reader in Religion,* ed. Carol P. Christ and Judith Plaskow (San Francisco: Harper & Row, 1979), a book containing excellent selections from other feminist religious thinkers as well. The distinction between "reformist" and "revolutionary" (or Christian and post-Christian) feminism is not hard and fast, and a number of women have moved across it or found themselves on the boundary.

55. Ruether, *Sexism and God-Talk,* 22; see chap. 1 on method.

56. Schüssler Fiorenza, *In Memory of Her,* 29–36. The 1st 3 chaps. discuss methodological questions in detail.

57. Ibid., chaps. 4–6.

58. Ibid., chap. 5.

59. Ibid., chap. 6; see the "apocryphal" letter of the apostle Phoebe quoted on pp. 61–64.

60. Ruether, *Women-Church,* 49–56.

61. In addition to *Women of Spirit,* ed. Ruether and McLaughlin, see Elizabeth A. Clark and Herbert Richardson, *Women and Religion: A Feminist Sourcebook of Christian Thought* (New York: Harper & Row, 1977); Elizabeth A. Clark, *Women in the Early Church* (Wilmington, Del.: Michael Glazier, 1983; Clark has also published monographs on Gerontius, John Chrysostom, and Faltonia Betitia Proba); Caroline Walker Bynum, *Jesus as Mother: Studies in the Spirituality of the High Middle Ages* (Berkeley and Los Angeles: Univ. of California Press, 1982); Dale A. Johnson, ed., *Women in English Religion: 1700–1925* (Lewiston, N.Y.: Edwin Mellen Press, 1983); and Rosemary Radford Ruether and Rosemary Skinner Keller, eds., *Women and Religion in America: A Documentary History* (San Francisco: Harper & Row, 1981–).

62. The discussion that follows is based on Ruether's *Women-Church,* intro. and part 1. See also the epilogue to Schüssler Fiorenza's *In Memory of Her.* Ruether provides a brief history of the women-church movement, on pp. 64–68. Although there are historical antecedents, the movement emerged in its present form in 1983, from the conference of the Women of the Church Coalition, which was a coalition of Catholic feminist movements. Women-church began as a Catholic movement because of the virtually total exclusion of women from leadership positions in the Roman Catholic church, except in women's religious orders. The very severity of the Catholic situation called for a radical response. The movement is, however, ecumenical and should include larger numbers of Protestant women, especially ordained Protestant women, who need the kind of support it provides just as urgently, because of the subtle, often unacknowledged sexism found in the Protestant churches.

63. Ruether uses this expression, and draws out the analogy to the Latin American situation, in *Sexism and God-Talk,* 201–6.

64. Ruether, *Women-Church,* 59–61.

65. See Paul Ricoeur, "Fatherhood: From Phantasm to Symbol," in *The Conflict of Interpretations* (Evanston, Ill.: Northwestern Univ. Press, 1974), 468–97.

66. See Sallie McFague, *Models of God: Theology for an Ecological, Nuclear Age* (Philadelphia: Fortress Press, 1987).

67. Wolfhart Pannenberg makes this point in *The Church,* trans. Keith Crim (Philadelphia: Westminster Press, 1983), chap. 10.

68. See ibid., chap. 6; and Hans Küng, *The Church* (New York: Image Books, 1976), 361–64.

69. At this point I am directly dependent on lectures presented by Peggy Way to the class at Vanderbilt on the church and its ministries. Way has been actively involved in ecumenical discussions for a number of years. I am also drawing on recent publications of the Consultation on Church Union: *The COCU Consensus: In Quest of a Church of Christ Uniting,* ed. Gerald F. Moede (Princeton, 1985); and *Covenanting toward Unity: From Consensus to Communion* (Princeton, 1985).

70. See Pannenberg, *The Church,* chap. 2; and the COCU documents cited in the preceding n.

71. The most informative studies are by Walbert Bühlmann (*The Coming of the Third Church: An Analysis of the Present and Future of the Church* [Maryknoll, N.Y.: Orbis Books, 1978]; *The Church of the Future: A Model for the Year 2001* [Maryknoll, N.Y.: Orbis Books, 1986]). The statistics in this thesis and the next are from *World Christian Encyclopedia,* ed. David B. Barrett (London: Oxford Univ. Press, 1982); see esp. the table on p. 6.

72. Curiously, the United States is the most religious and the most secular of cultures at one and the same time. At the beginning of *Habits of the Heart,* Robert Bellah and his colleagues provide portraits of four typical Americans, three of whom seem to be utterly without religious commitments or sensibilities; yet statistics show that some forty percent of Americans attend weekly religious services (far higher than in most other Western nations), and religious membership is around sixty percent of the total population. See Robert N. Bellah et al., *Habits of the Heart: Individualism and Commitment in American Life* (Berkeley and Los Angeles: Univ. of California Press, 1985), 3–20, 219.

73. Of a growing number of recent books published on this subject, two of the most important are John Hick's *God Has Many Names* (Philadelphia: Westminster Press, 1982) and Paul F. Knitter's *No Other Name? A Critical Survey of Christian Attitudes toward the World Religions* (Maryknoll, N.Y.: Orbis Books, 1985). I am also relying on a report by Knitter of the conference "Christology and World Religions" held at the Claremont Graduate School, March 7–8, 1986.

74. The habit is preserved by evangelical Protestantism but in a modified form that legitimates strategies of mission and conversion but no longer of conflict and persecution.

75. The inclusivist theory has its roots in Hegel's philosophy of religion (although strictly speaking Hegel offers a typology rather than a developmental history of religions) and has been widely espoused by 19th-cent. liberal Protestantism and 20th-cent. Catholicism, of which Karl Rahner was a distinguished spokesperson.

76. This position was first articulated by Ernst Troeltsch at the end of his career (see "Christianity among World Religions," in *Christian Thought*), but it was almost universally rejected. Now it is the view shared by Knitter, Hick, Wilfrid Cantwell Smith, John Cobb, Langdon Gilkey, Gordon Kaufman, David Tracy, Raymond Panikkar, Stanley Samartha,

and many others, despite individual differences. See the readings in *Christianity and Other Religions,* ed. John Hick and Brian Hebblethwaite (Philadelphia: Fortress Press, 1981).

77. John B. Cobb, Jr., *Beyond Dialogue: Toward a Mutual Transformation of Christianity and Buddhism* (Philadelphia: Fortress Press, 1982), esp. 47–52, 141–43, and chaps. 4 and 5.

3. TOWARD A THEOLOGY OF MINISTRY IN THE NEW PARADIGM

1. Of particular help to me have been H. Richard Niebuhr, *The Purpose of the Church and Its Ministry: Reflections on the Aims of Theological Education* (New York: Harper & Bros., 1956); Bernard Cooke, *Ministry to Word and Sacraments: History and Theology* (Philadelphia: Fortress Press, 1976); Edward Schillebeeckx, *Ministry: Leadership in the Community of Jesus Christ* (New York: Crossroad, 1981), issued in a revised and expanded version as *The Church with a Human Face* (New York: Crossroad, 1985); Dieter T. Hessel, *Social Ministry* (Philadelphia: Westminster Press, 1982); and Rosemary Radford Ruether, *Women-Church: Theology and Practice of Feminist Liturgical Communities* (San Francisco: Harper & Row, 1985), esp. chap. 5. I have also benefited from discussions with colleagues, esp. Liston Mills, Donald Beisswenger, and David Buttrick.

2. This is the basic thesis of Cooke's *Ministry to Word and Sacraments;* see esp. part 1.

3. The Pauline image (2 Cor. 4:7) is adopted by James Gustafson, in *Treasure in Earthen Vessels: The Church as a Human Community* (New York: Harper & Bros., 1961).

4. Thus Schillebeeckx in the book of this title (*Ministry: Leadership in the Community of Jesus Christ*). Leadership is essentially what Niebuhr has in mind when "for want of a better phrase," he refers to the "new idea" of the minister as a "pastoral director" (*The Purpose of the Church and Its Ministry,* 79–91). "Leadership," in my view, *is* a better phrase, since it is not dominated by administrative or managerial associations.

5. I am opposed not to the idea of a call as such but to its not uncommon abuse in Protestant churches when it is assumed that one *must* have an identifiable and direct personal call, and when the claim to have such a call is allowed to certify one as competent for ministry. On the idea of the call to ministry, see Niebuhr, *Purpose of the Church,* 63–66.

6. See Cooke, *Ministry to Word and Sacraments,* chaps. 1 and 2; Schillebeeckx, *Ministry,* chaps. 1 and 2; and idem, *The Church with a Human Face,* parts 1 and 2.

7. Ruether, *Women-Church,* 75.

8. Horace Bushnell, *Christian Nurture* (New York: Charles Scribner's Sons, 1886), 9, 65. The ostrich, Bushnell observes, "hatches her young without incubation, depositing her eggs in the sand to be quickened by the solar heat."

9. Paul Ricoeur, *The Symbolism of Evil,* trans. Emerson Buchanan (Boston: Beacon Press, 1969), 19, 352.

10. See pp. 76–77 above.

Index

USBORNE BEGI...

VOLCANOES

Stephanie Turnbull
Designed by Nancy Leschnikoff
Illustrated by Andy Tudor

Volcano consultant: Professor Gillian Foulger,
Department of Earth Sciences, University of Durham
Reading consultant: Alison Kelly, Roehampton University
Additional illustrations by Tim Haggerty

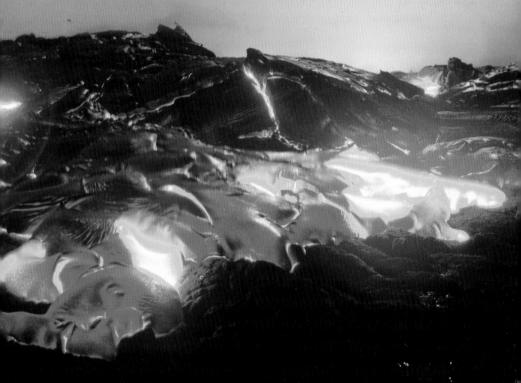

Contents

Exploding Earth

There are thousands of volcanoes around the world. Some spray red-hot melted rock called lava. Others blast out clouds of ash.

This is Mount Etna on Sicily shooting out lava.

A volcano forms

The Earth has an outer shell called the crust.
Underneath this is a thick layer of hot rock
called the mantle.

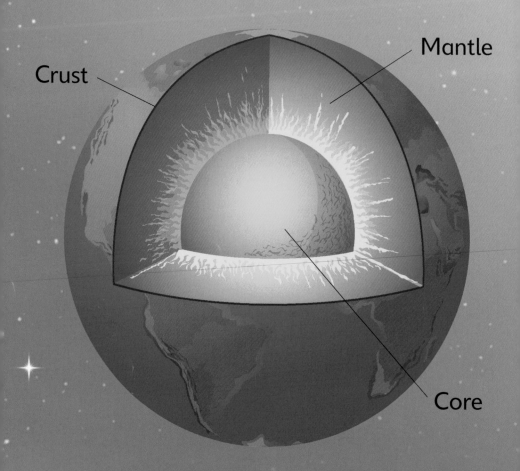

Crust

Mantle

Core

The middle of the Earth is called the core.
It is made of extremely hot metal.

There are cracks in the crust. Hot rock melts and pushes up into the cracks.

Melted rock

The melted rock builds up and bursts out as lava. This is called an eruption.

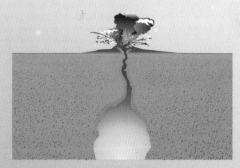

The lava hardens into rock. Layers of lava build up after many eruptions.

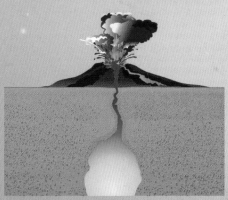

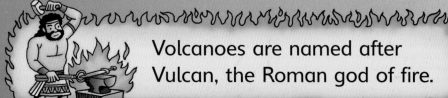

Volcanoes are named after Vulcan, the Roman god of fire.

Fiery fountains

Some lava is runny, so gas
inside it bubbles out easily.
This creates gentle eruptions.

This is Piton de la Fournaise,
on the island of Réunion.
Runny lava sprays out
of it like a fountain.

Runny lava is like thin honey or hot wax.
It gushes down the sides of the volcano.

The lava spreads a long way before
it cools and hardens.

A volcano with gently sloping
sides slowly builds up.

The tallest lava
fountain ever was five
times higher than the
Eiffel Tower in Paris.

Big blasts

Some volcanoes have thick lava that is full of gas bubbles. The gas makes lava burst out in a violent eruption.

Clouds of ash and big lumps of lava blast into the air.

Some lumps of lava are jagged rocks called blocks.

Other lumps cool into long, twisted shapes called bombs.

Some blocks of lava are as big as trucks.

Red-hot rivers

Lava that flows from an erupting volcano is much, much hotter than boiling water.

This glowing lava river sets fire to all the trees, plants and buildings it reaches.

Thick lava moves slowly, which gives people and animals time to escape.

Thick lava breaks into rough chunks as it cools down.

Runny lava sets into smooth, swirly shapes instead.

Deadly clouds

Violent eruptions throw out thick clouds of ash, rocks and gas. These clouds sweep down the volcano's slopes.

This terrifying ash cloud came from Mount Pinatubo in the Philippines in 1991. It covered the land all around with a thick blanket of ash.

Sometimes snow and ice on top of high volcanoes melt and mix with the hot ash.

The muddy mixture gushes down the volcano like a river of hot, wet concrete.

Clouds of ash, rocks and gas move faster than a racing car.

Undersea eruptions

Many volcanoes form under the sea.
They erupt gently and lava cools quickly
in the water.

1. An underwater
volcano grows taller
as it keeps erupting.

2. When it reaches
the water's surface,
clouds of steam rise.

3. Soon the top of
the volcano sticks
up out of the sea.

4. The lava keeps
building up and
forms an island.

This photograph taken from space shows the island of Hawaii.

Hawaii was formed by underwater volcanoes.

The dark area in the middle of the island is Mauna Loa, the world's biggest volcano.

Underwater lava can harden into round rocks called pillow lava.

Hot water

The melted rock underneath a volcano heats up the ground around it.

The hot ground also heats up any rain that soaks into it.

Heated water bubbles out and forms a hot spring.

In Iceland, hot spring water is used in swimming pools.

These snow monkeys are keeping warm in a steaming hot spring. The spring is high in the mountains of Japan and is heated by the Shiga Kogen volcano.

Black smokers

Hot springs called black smokers can form around underwater volcanoes.

Black smokers are jets of dark, cloudy water.

Tiny grains in the water build up to form tall chimneys.

Tubeworms and shrimps feed on the cloudy water around black smokers.

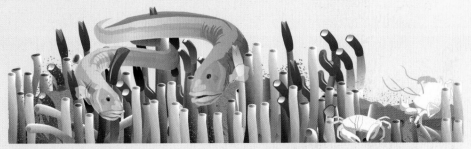

Crabs and long fish called eelpouts also live there, eating smaller animals.

Sometimes a deep sea octopus visits black smokers to search for food.

Some springs blow out pale clouds of water. They are called white smokers.

Great geysers

Sometimes water heated by a volcano shoots out of the ground with a cloud of steam. This is called a geyser.

Here you can see Old Faithful Geyser in Yellowstone National Park, USA.

Boiling water blasts out of the ground every hour.

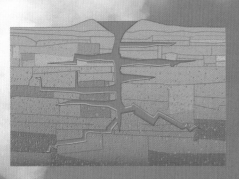

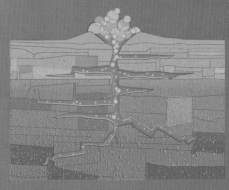

1. Rainwater gets trapped in lots of tiny cracks in the ground.

2. Hot volcanic rock heats the water until it fizzes and boils.

3. The boiling water bursts out into the air with a whoosh.

4. It soaks back into the cracks and starts to heat up again.

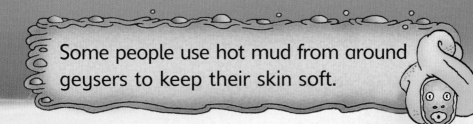

Some people use hot mud from around geysers to keep their skin soft.

Dead or alive?

Volcanoes that are erupting or could erupt in the future are alive. Ones that will never erupt again are dead or extinct.

This is Mount Popa, an extinct volcano in Burma. A temple stands on the top.

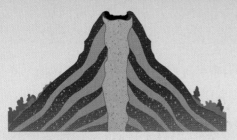

A volcano can become extinct if hard lava plugs its main tube or vent.

Over many years the volcano's sides wear away, leaving the lava plug.

Some volcanoes don't erupt for thousands of years, but they are not dead – only sleeping.

ZZZZZ

Violent Vesuvius

One of the worst eruptions ever was that of Mount Vesuvius in Italy, 2,000 years ago.

Ash and rocks from the volcano rained down on a nearby town called Pompeii.

Some people hurried away from the town, but others hid in their homes instead.

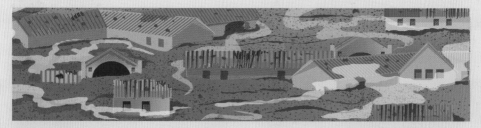

Later that day, Pompeii was buried in a river of mud and ash that set hard, like cement.

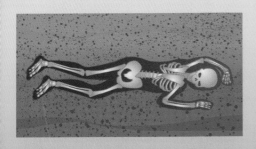

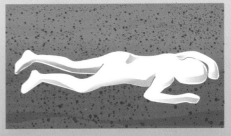

Years later, experts found holes in the rock left by bodies that rotted away.

They filled the holes with plaster, then cut away the rock to see the body shapes.

This is a plaster model of a man who was choked to death by ash.

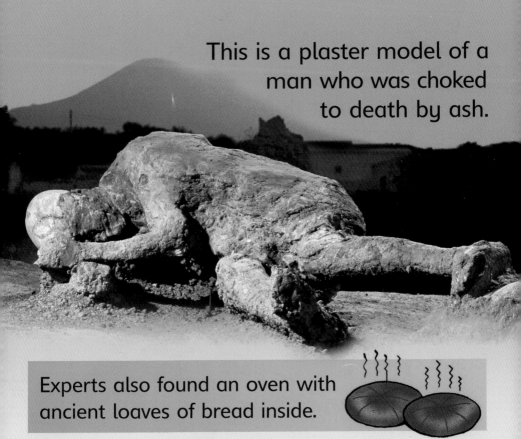

Experts also found an oven with ancient loaves of bread inside.

American eruption

In 1980, the high, snow-covered peak of Mount St. Helens in the USA was blasted away in an enormous eruption.

This is what Mount St. Helens looked like in the years before it erupted.

Then one side of the volcano began to swell up and the ground shook.

Suddenly the volcano's side exploded in a cloud of ash and rocks.

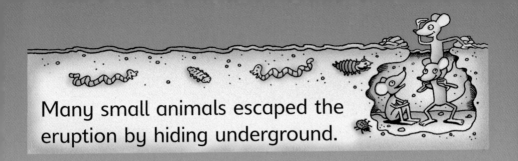

Many small animals escaped the eruption by hiding underground.

This is how Mount St. Helens looked after the eruption. Part of the volcano was gone, and the land around was destroyed.

The volcano began rumbling again in 2004. Another eruption may be on the way.

Volcano experts

Volcanologists are people who study volcanoes and predict when they will erupt.

This volcanologist is using a machine that senses changes in ground level.

A bulge on a volcano's slope could mean melted rock is pushing up inside.

A volcano may give off lots of gas before it erupts, so experts take gas samples.

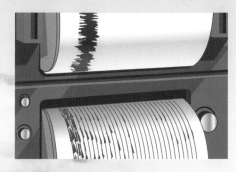

The ground may also shake before an eruption. A machine records this shaking.

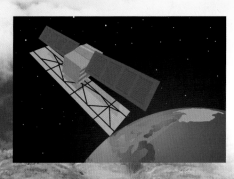

Photographs taken by satellites in space show any changes in the volcano's shape.

Some people think that animals can sense when a volcano is about to erupt.

Glossary of volcano words

Here are some of the words in this book you might not know. This page tells you what they mean.

 lava - melted rock that has erupted from a volcano.

 spring - water that flows out of the ground.

 tubeworm - a long, red-tipped worm that attaches itself to the sea floor.

 geyser - a spring that shoots a jet of steaming hot water out of the ground.

 extinct - dead. An extinct volcano is one that will never erupt again.

 volcanologist - a scientist who studies volcanoes.

 satellite - a machine in space that takes pictures of the Earth's surface.

Websites to visit

If you have a computer, you can find out more about volcanoes on the Internet. On the Usborne Quicklinks website there are links to four fun websites.

Website 1 - Watch short video clips of volcanoes erupting.

Website 2 - Explore an underwater spring.

Website 3 - Try a volcano quiz.

Website 4 - Play a movie to find out more about how volcanoes form.

To visit these websites, go to **www.usborne-quicklinks.com** and type the keywords "beginners volcanoes". Then click on the link for the website you want to visit. Before you use the Internet, look at the safety guidelines inside the back cover of this book and ask an adult to read them with you.

This is Mount Etna, the largest volcano in Europe.

Index

Acknowledgements

Photographic manipulation by Mike Wheatley, Nick Wakeford and John Russell
With thanks to Rosie Dickins and Catriona Clarke

Photo credits

The publishers are grateful to the following for permission to reproduce material:
© Age Fotostock/Powerstock 6-7; © Corbis 12-13 (Alberto Garcia), 22-23 (Christophe Loviny),
25 (Roger Ressmeyer); © Getty Images Cover (Ezio Geneletti), 1 (Richard A Cooke III), 31 (Art Wolfe);
© Mauritius/Powerstock 8-9; © NASA/Science Photo Library 15; © National Geographic/Getty Images 20-21
(Norbert Rosing); © PhotoLink/Getty Images 27; © Reuters/Corbis 10-11 (Tony Gentile);
© Science Photo Library 16-17 (Akira Uchiyama); © Still Pictures 2-3 (Otto Hahn);
© University of Victoria 18 (Dr Verena Tunnicliffe); © USGS 28-29 (Mike Poland).

Every effort has been made to trace and acknowledge ownership of copyright. If any rights have
been omitted, the publishers offer to rectify this in any subsequent editions following notification.